MW00654311

Victory Decrees

DESTINY IMAGE BOOKS BY JENNIFER LECLAIRE

The Spiritual Warrior's Guide to Defeating Water Spirits
The Seer Dimensions

Victory Decrees

Daily Prophetic Strategies for Spiritual Warfare Victory

JENNIFER LECLAIRE

DESTINY IMAGE® PUBLISHERS, INC.
P.O. Box 310, Shippensburg, PA 17257-0310
"Promoting Inspired Lives."

This book and all other Destiny Image and Destiny Image Fiction books are available at Christian bookstores and distributors worldwide.

Cover design by Eileen Rockwell
Interior design by Terry Clifton

For more information on foreign distributors, call 717-532-3040.
Reach us on the Internet: www.destinyimage.com.

ISBN 13 TP: 978-0-7684-5149-8
ISBN 13 eBook: 978-0-7684-5147-4
ISBN 13 HC: 978-0-7684-5146-7
ISBN 13 LP: 978-0-7684-5148-1

For Worldwide Distribution, Printed in the U.S.A.
2 3 4 5 6 7 8 / 23 22 21 20 19

Dedication

I dedicate this book to the prayer warriors who help lift up my hands in the battle, the intercessors at PrayerforJennifer.com, who make up the hedge of protection and are the watchman on the wall who look out over my life. The list is too long to name you all, but I could not do what I do without Vanessa Angelini, Christine Jackman, Pilar Barido, and Dallamys Olazabal. Toni Lynn Alloway and Karen Ledbetter, thanks for transcribing my prophetic words so the nations can read them again and again.

Content

Foreword

*I*n every generation, there arises distinct prophetic voices that redirect the hearts and minds of the Christian community back to God. It is my opinion that Jennifer LeClaire is one of those voices. An anointed and prolific communicator of truth, Jennifer helps us to lean into God through prayer, stand up for God through biblically based decrees, and prepares us to give an answer for the hope that is within in us. (See First Peter 3:15.) *Victory Decrees* is a significant contribution to the conversation surrounding spiritual warfare; it elevates the Word of God as the believer's divine agency to safeguarding the mind, empowering the spirit, and healing the soul. Every believer must come to a place of maturity wherein he or she relies on God's Word, "in order that Satan might not outwit us. For we are not unaware of his schemes" (2 Corinthians 2:11 NIV). *Victory Decrees* is filled with the types of prayer strategies that are so vital to the life of a believer as it relates to winning spiritual battles.

Imagine a series of intimate conversations that unveiled the heart of God—that provided a prolific perspective concerning the root cause, ultimate intention, and specific configuration of the enemy's overt and covert plans to destroy your destiny. How much more successful would you be in living your life proactively and offensively, rather than reactively and defensively? Further imagine receiving an indispensable, Spirit-inspired directive on what your posture should be in order to obtain victory in all areas of your life, and to flourish wherever God has planted you according to Psalms 1:3; 72:7-9; 92:12-15. This is the essence of *Victory Decrees*. The practical nature of this manual fills in the gaps typically left by the more general spiritual warfare approaches of our time. It is an innovative work and should be required reading for the emerging generation of Christians who are battling more deviant, deceptive, and insidious battles, as well as the enduring satanic concentrations of stealth-mode attacks. *Victory Decrees* is a blueprint for biblical success, and takes seriously the divine dictum, "Thou shalt also decree a thing, and it shall be established unto thee: and light shall shine upon thy ways" (Job 22:28 KJV).

This book is a page-turning missive. In this devotional-style repository, you will be empowered with a daily scripture to meditate on, a succinct prayer in which to gain prayer mastery, and a decree that reinforces your spiritual authority. Although written in a manner that gives the reader a daily dose of inspiration and empowerment, I could not put the manuscript down and found myself reading page after page until, on the first sitting, I had read an entire month's worth of declarations!

It is my prayer that *Victory Decrees* will captivate you as it did me—and then usher you into a new dimension and realm that gives you the authority and power to overcome the spiritual battles waged against you. May this work guide you to a place where you sense the presence of the Spirit of God advising you as He exposes the tactics of the enemy. Many times, the methods, strategies, and tactics of the warfare we encounter—and the specific agents used against us—become a clarifying key to the path we should take in fulfilling our greater destiny, because the enemy fights us in the area he fears us most. So take heart! As you devote your time to absorbing the long overdue and significant revelations within *Victory Decrees*, God will give you a greater understanding of His plans for your life as you take your place in the Kingdom of Heaven, wielding the Word of God as your ultimate weapon of warfare.

Dr. Cindy Trimm
Life Strategist, Bestselling Author, Humanitarian

Introduction

*W*hen I accepted Christ into my life, I didn't realize I was stepping into an epic spiritual war. No one told me saying yes to Jesus was akin to enrolling as a soldier in the army of God. I didn't have the first clue about spiritual armor; weapons of warfare; keys to the Kingdom for binding and loosing; spirits of Jezebel, witchcraft, python; or anything else.

Simply put, I was ignorant of the devil's devices.

Needless to say, it didn't take me long to start looking into scriptures such as First Peter 5:8, Second Corinthians 10:4–5, and Ephesians 6:12. Jesus told us the enemy comes to kill, steal, and destroy, but He came to give us a life of abundant overflow (see John 10:10). He left us His peace, His joy, and His provision—His Word, His Spirit, His blood, and His name. But despite who we are in Christ—or perhaps because of who we are in Christ—the war against our body and soul rages.

Many years ago when I found myself on a new level of warfare—a level at which I had not operated—the Holy Spirit said something to me that seemed rather obvious.

"You are in a war," He said.

"Yes," I replied. "I know that. And I feel like I am losing."

Yes, I knew I was in a war but sometimes we're too quick to dismiss enemy interference as happenstance. In our dialogue the Holy Spirit was reminding me that the war in the unseen realm is raging. There are spiritual bombs that devastate lives, spiritual spies and saboteurs, air strikes and ground strikes, and the like. The war will not end until Christ comes back for the grand finale, but we can walk in victory despite unseen forces aiming to wreak havoc on our lives.

The first key to consistent victory is understanding that we war from a place of absolute triumph. The Bible says we are seated in heavenly places in Christ Jesus (see Ephesians 2:6). The Bible says that Jesus is the head of the church, and we are the body (see Colossians 1:18). The Bible says Jesus is far above all principalities and powers (see Ephesians 1:21).

That means, legally, the devil is far below our feet, and we are given authority to keep him there. We enforce the victory Christ won over the principalities and powers. This can be tough to remember when the onslaught hits our minds, our finances, our relationships, and our bodies.

That's why I wrote this devotional, *Victory Decrees*. Well, I should say the Holy Spirit wrote it. The pages of this devotional contain wisdom, cautions, and encouragement for spiritual warfare by the Holy Spirit. At times you'll say "amen" and at times you might say "ouch," but it's a good ouch. It's the kind of ouch that wakes us up to see a better way to war when it looks like you're losing the battle. It's the kind of ouch that presses us to prepare for the battle coming down the pike.

Victory Decrees is my first spiritual warfare devotional, following the popular volumes *Mornings With the Holy Spirit* and *Evenings With the Holy Spirit* that have been translated into several languages and read around the world. Through my *Mornings With the Holy Spirit* daily prayer broadcast on Facebook and Periscope, these devotionals have reached believers in almost every nation. During these broadcasts, I often prophesy and engage in spiritual warfare. In fact, many of the prophecies in this book came directly from prophecies I released on the broadcast that my staff chronicled.

After writing many, many books on the practical aspects and theology of spiritual warfare, I decided to write a devotional filled with the Holy Spirit's inspiration for those fighting, along with Scriptures to study, prayers to pray, and decrees and declarations to release over your life. If you'll engage with the Holy Spirit daily, hear His words, pray these prayers, and follow the wisdom of these Scriptures, you'll grow stronger day by day by day.

That's my prayer for you. I hate seeing the enemy gain ground in the lives of believers. He does so many times because we are ignorant of the devil's devices. He does so as we advance to new levels and haven't found our footing yet in the new place. He does so through old enemies that we didn't fully defeat in the past seasons. He does so in many ways.

In this devotional the Holy Spirit reveals some of His ways and the enemy's ways so that you can walk like Christ in the earth, destroying the work of the devil. Remember, you win!

JANUARY

Do not remember the former things, nor consider the things of old. Behold, I will do a new thing, now it shall spring forth; shall you not know it? I will even make a road in the wilderness and rivers in the desert. The beast of the field will honor Me, the jackals and the ostriches, because I give waters in the wilderness and rivers in the desert, to give drink to My people, My chosen. This people I have formed for Myself; they shall declare My praise.

ISAIAH 43:18–21

Break Demonic Cycles in Your Life

You don't have to repeat the same cycles this year that you walked in last year. You can break demonic cycles in your life. You don't have to walk in the same vicious, painful, distressing circles this year. You can interrupt the enemy's plans, but first you have to be aware of the enemy's involvement. You have to see how the wicked one is working to press your buttons, to bring up old memories, to strike at opportune times. You can start this year with a new determination to overcome what has tried over and again to overcome you. I am with you.

2 Corinthians 10:3–6; Matthew 4:17; John 8:32

PRAYER

Father, help me discern the destructive demonic cycles that manifest in my life. And give me the strategy to overcome every wicked plot against my life.

DECREE

I decree the enemy's plans in my life are disrupted, dismantled, and disengaged. I declare demonic cycles are obliterated, in Jesus's name.

Winning the Battle in the Wilderness

There will always be a battle in the wilderness—and it's twofold. You'll have to battle your carnal nature that grows impatient in the waiting. You'll be tempted to take matters into your own hands to bring change into your life that only I can bring. You'll grow weary in the waiting if you don't keep your eyes on Jesus. But your enemy will add another dimension of warfare to your wilderness experience, taking advantage of your impatience and weariness to tempt you to give up altogether. Your promised land is ahead. Join Me in the war against your flesh and against the enemy of your soul.

MATTHEW 4:1–11; HEBREWS 6:12; GALATIANS 6:9

PRAYER

Father, I will walk through any wilderness You lead me into, but please keep me from temptation. Help me to walk and not grow weary.

DECREE

I decree I am strong in the Lord and in the power of His might. I declare I am able to walk through any wilderness through His grace and by His mercy, in Jesus's name.

Your Enemy Is Not Impenetrable

Goliath had a helmet of bronze, a coat of mail, and a bronze spear between his shoulders. This giant—this enemy—seemed impenetrable. But I tell you, your enemy's armor is not impenetrable. Your enemy is no match for the sword of the Spirit. Your enemy actually has no armor. Your enemy is vulnerable to the Word of God coming out of your mouth. But your mind is penetrable in the unrenewed areas. Your mind is the point of entry where your enemies make you think and even believe that their armor is impenetrable. David knew his God, ran to the battle line, and saw victory. You can too.

1 SAMUEL 17:48–49; 1 CHRONICLES 29:10–13; ISAIAH 26:3

PRAYER

Thank You, Lord, that You have given me stronger armor than any Goliath could hope for. Help me see myself as I am in Christ. Help me see the victory beyond the enemy's intimidation.

DECREE

I decree and declare every Goliath in my life shall fall flat on his face. I decree victory over every giant overshadowing God's blessings in my life, in Jesus's name.

Submitting to Me Means Resisting the Enemy

*W*hen you don't resist the devil's plans, plots, and ploys against your life, you are not submitting yourself to Me. I have given you strong and sage advice and instruction in My Word. I have told you plainly to submit yourself to My Spirit, resist enemy spirits and they will flee from you.

When you don't resist fear, when you don't cast down vain imaginations, when you don't resist demon powers in their various workings against your life, you are resisting My wisdom. So, resist the enemy at his onset. Don't wait until oppression washes over you. I will always deliver you from the enemy's hand when you obey My Word. Resist.

JAMES 4:7; 1 PETER 5:9; MATTHEW 16:23

PRAYER

Lord, thank You for this revelation that submitting to You and resisting the devil work hand in hand. Give me the strength to resist with everything in me and not cave into the pressure.

DECREE

I decree I have the power and might of God within me to resist every enemy attack. I declare that oppression is broken off my mind and body, in Jesus's name!

Believe My Promises of Provision

*B*lessed are the poor in spirit, but I have not called you to walk with less than enough. I am the God of more than enough. I have more than enough provision, and I want to pour it out upon you liberally. Your part is to believe My great and precious promises of provision over your life. Your part is to fight the good fight of faith over your finances. Your part is to bind the hand of the thief who comes to steal, kill, and destroy. Your part is to keep your mouth in line with My Word and stop talking about what you don't have. Your part is to put your hand to the plow and give Me something to bless. Don't be deceived. I am your provider.

2 CORINTHIANS 9:8; JOB 38:41; LUKE 12:7

PRAYER

Father, I believe. Help my unbelief when the enemy is filling my head with thoughts of lack. I bind the voice and the hand of the enemy over my finances!

DECREE

I decree my God has more than enough resources to provide all my needs. I declare that all my needs are met—and then some, in Jesus's name!

January 6

I Need Your Undivided Attention

I long to sit with you—to hide you under the shadow of My wings day and night. If you will just give me a few minutes, I can change your life. I can change your perspective. I can change your thoughts. I can teach you things. I can show you things. But I need your undivided attention. I've authorized mercy for you. I've authorized prayer answers for you. The enemy wants to steal away the answers and delay the answers. I see the distractions and the enemy interference. It's like static on a radio that makes it difficult to hear the message. Sit with Me and My voice will rise above the static, and you will hear the answers the enemy has been working to keep from you.

PROVERBS 2:2–5; ISAIAH 26:3; LAMENTATIONS 3:25

PRAYER

Father, I give You my time and I give You my heart. Help me to overcome the distractions that work like little foxes to spoil my vine and my time with You.

DECREE

I decree that the enemy's static is silenced, and God's transmissions reach my heart. I declare that God is answering my prayers and delay is broken over my life, in Jesus's name.

Deploy My Joy as a Weapon

*M*y joy is your strength. My joy is a strong weapon. Deploy My joy against the discouragement that attacks your soul. Deploy My joy unspeakable and full of glory against the darkness that tries to overtake you. Deploy My joy against the depression that wants to sideline you from your destiny. My joy is within you. Let the river of joy flow from within you and overwhelm the enemies that want to bring you down and take you out.

ROMANS 15:13; PHILIPPIANS 4:4; PROVERBS 17:22

PRAYER

Father, thank You for your joy unspeakable and full of glory. Help me to deploy your joy in the face of every enemy attack so I can stand strong and sing Your song.

DECREE

I decree the joy I express in the Lord will overwhelm the enemy's plans and send confusion into his camp. I decree I am wading through the river of the joy of the Lord, in Jesus's name.

When the Enemy Is Breathing Down Your Neck

*W*hen you feel the enemy breathing down your neck, keep running the race. Demons work to intimidate you, to harass you, and to deceive you. Their hot breath on your neck can make it seem like they could strike you down at any moment. In that moment refuse to focus on the enemy behind you and intentionally focus on the God inside of you. Draw near to Me, and I will draw near to you. Then you will feel the sweet peace of My Spirit and a fresh wind of My anointing that overshadows the enemy's hot breath on your neck.

HEBREWS 12:1–3; EXODUS 33:14; ACTS 2:1–4

PRAYER

Father, the enemy's breath seems to have a voice. Help me to embrace the wind of Your Spirit when the enemy is huffing and puffing at my back.

DECREE

I decree that I outpace every enemy force, like Elijah outpaced Ahab after the showdown at Mount Carmel. I declare the wind of Your Spirit is at my back, empowering me, in Jesus's name.

Tap Into the Anointing to War

Jesus was anointed and went about doing good and healing all who were oppressed of the devil. He had an anointing to heal, but He also had an anointing to war. He used that anointing for war to do good, not evil. Many times, you will encounter people who are doing you wrong, who are visiting you with evil intentions. Use your warfare anointing to return good for evil and you will be like Jesus, your Savior. Return good for evil and trust Me to bring vindication. I am the warrior, but I don't fight like the world fights. Neither should you.

ACTS 10:38; EXODUS 15:3; ISAIAH 42:13

PRAYER

Father, help me remember the anointing for war is not meant to be aimed toward people but demon powers. Teach me to war like You war and to love like You love.

DECREE

I decree Christ's anointing operating in my life destroys the works of darkness at every turn. I declare I fight like my heavenly Father fights, in Jesus's name.

Discern the Voice Speaking to You

*P*aul the apostle explained there are many voices in the spirit. John the apostle later warned you not to believe every spirit, but to test them. There are many spirits in the world, and they all have something to say. They all have an assignment. Vain imaginations are a vehicle for that assignment. Jesus warned to be careful how you listen. Listen closely to the thoughts that enter your mind. They are not all My thoughts, and they are not all your thoughts. The enemy's voice travels in the form of a thought. Judge your thoughts, test the spirits, discern the voice. This is a key to winning the battle in your mind.

1 CORINTHIANS 14:10; 1 JOHN 4:1; MARK 4:24

PRAYER

Father, help me not to be deceived by voices that mimic yours, twist truth into lies, and try to lead me astray. Help me to discern the many voices in the spirit.

DECREE

I decree every counterfeit voice working to infiltrate my soul is shut out and shut up. I declare I hear the voice of the Holy Spirit and cast down every other whisper, in Jesus's name.

Embrace the Spirit of Cooperation

Don't fight and war with your brothers and sisters over titles and promotions and other blessings. Where there is unity, I will command a blessing that you cannot contain. I will command a blessing that forces you to cooperate with another to reap that harvest because there is more than enough for all My children. Dare to believe Me today and to stretch yourself further than you did yesterday. Understand and know you can overcome whatever is facing you down when you work with your spiritual family. You will overcome together.

PSALM 133; NEHEMIAH 4:6; EPHESIANS 4:3

PRAYER

Father, help me to honor my brothers and sisters in Christ. Help me to help them do what they are called to do and avoid all striving, for Your glory.

DECREE

I decree strife cannot make its way into my relationships. I declare I am one with my brothers and sisters in the Lord, and we will accomplish great things together, in Jesus's name.

Loose Yourself from the Spirit of Infirmity

The spirit of infirmity is sneaky. It will come to attack from time to time, bringing sickness and disease and strange ailments for which the doctors can't find solid diagnoses and can't seem to cure. But I am the God who heals you and removes sickness from you. I am the One who paid the price for your complete healing so you can walk in divine health. I am the One who has the power to drive the spirit of infirmity away from you as you command it to loose you, in Jesus's name.

EXODUS 23:25; PSALM 91:10; PSALM 103:3

PRAYER

Father, thank You for Your healing power that works in me. Thank You for providing a way of escape from the spirit of infirmity by Your blood.

DECREE

I decree the spirit of infirmity must flee from me now! I declare sickness and disease dies when it comes in contact with my body, for His glory, in Jesus's name.

Wage War with the Prophetic Word

When you look back at the prophetic words I have released over your life, you'll know better how to fight what is attacking you in the next season. The words I speak to you are spirit and life. Fight the enemy's resistance with those words. Those prophecies that came from My heart over your life will invigorate you in the battle. They will arm you for war against the specific assignment the enemy has launched against you. They will strengthen your arms to lift up your shield of faith. They are revelation for you to war with. Look back at the prophetic words, and the season you are in will make more sense.

1 TIMOTHY 1:18; 2 CHRONICLES 20:20

PRAYER

Father, remind me of the prophetic words I've long ago forgotten about. Arm me with the revelation of Your will for my life so I can stand in faith without wavering.

DECREE

I decree every prophetic word spoken over my life shall come to pass, despite enemy resistance. I declare God's words over me shall not return void, in Jesus's name.

Determine to Fight the Good Fight

I've called you to be an agent of change in the earth but change never comes without resistance. The enemy will always resist My light, My life, and My love manifesting through you to a dark, hopeless, hateful world. The enemy will resist you directly as you work with My Spirit to bring the truth to the people I love. But rest assured in this: as you determine to fight the good fight of faith, the resistance will make you stronger. So, get determined, resist the resistance. I will strengthen you to fight if you determine you're willing.

1 Timothy 6:12; James 4:7; Matthew 5:16

PRAYER

Father, help me resist the resistance. Strengthen me in my inner man to stand and withstand in the evil day. I am willing to stand against the wiles of the enemy.

DECREE

I decree every resistance to God's good, perfect, and acceptable will must bow to Jesus. I declare I am a change agent in the earth, empowered by the Holy Spirit, in Jesus's name.

Beware of Spiritual Warfare Ditches

*I*t so grieves Me how some of My children refuse to believe in the existence of the evil one when My Word of truth points to his work over and over again. But it also grieves me when my children fail to see the victory Christ won for them when He shamed principalities and powers through the work of the cross. There are two great deceptions in the earth My beloved ones fall into. They ignore the enemy, or they cower to his fearful agendas. Don't let that be you. Understand the reality of your enemy but understand I have given you victory over every spiritual foe in the name of Jesus. Remember that when his attack rages against you and strengthen your brothers and sisters.

1 PETER 5:8; COLOSSIANS 2:15; 2 CORINTHIANS 2:11

PRAYER

Father, please warn me if I am in danger of falling into one of these ditches. Help me focus on the victory I have over the enemy, but never underestimating my foes.

DECREE

I decree the enemy is trapped in his own deceptive ditch of lies. I declare my victory over the powers of darkness and subtle deceptions that try to find a way into my soul, in Jesus's name.

January 16

Receive a War Strategy that Shocks the Enemy

*J*ust as Father was with Jesus, He is with you. And your Father in Heaven is a master strategist. No enemy attack takes Him by surprise. No whispered lie the wicked one releases convinces Him to leave you. Yes, the devil is the accuser of the brethren, and he accuses you to Father. He accuses Father to you. He accuses you to yourself, and he causes you to look for someone to blame for your warfare. Don't fall into this demonic trap. Turn to your Father in Heaven for a strategy of war that will surprise the enemy of your soul. You cannot lose.

JOHN 17:20; REVELATION 12:10; HEBREWS 13:5

PRAYER

Father, thank You for standing with me in battle. Help me avoid the temptation to point fingers at You or anybody else when I am under attack. Give me a strategy to overcome.

DECREE

I decree the accuser of the brethren is cast down from my heart and mind. I declare my battle plan will shock the enemy and cause him to flee, in Jesus's name.

January 17

Put on Christ

*I*t's good that you have put on your whole armor, but you also need to put on Christ. Walk in Him. Walk in a revelation of who He is in you and who you are in Him. When you put on Christ and determine in your heart to align your character with His, you will maintain an authority over the wicked one. When you put on Christ and walk in Him, low-level devils that derailed you in past seasons will not attempt to harass you. And when the higher-ranking spirits launch fiery darts against you, you will laugh at your enemies just like your Father in Heaven because you know nothing shall by any means harm you.

GALATIANS 3:27; 2 PETER 3:18; ROMANS 8:5

PRAYER

Father, thank You for equipping me with spiritual armor to fight my battles. Help me not neglect to get dressed for war against armed and dangerous spirits.

DECREE

I decree my armor—the armor God Himself gave me—hinders hindering spirits targeting me. I declare I have put on Christ and I walk in Him every day and at all times, in Jesus's name.

Love Can Work as a Weapon

*U*se love as an advantage over your adversary. Love can work as a weapon for you in the spiritual battle. For although you are ultimately wrestling demons in the spirit world, the enemy often works through people to harm you with lies, accusations, and other harmful words. Walk in love. Overcome evil with good. Buy a gift for the one the enemy has stirred against you or offer a sincere compliment. In doing so, you will heap coals of Holy Spirit's conviction on their head, and you can both walk in freedom.

GALATIANS 5:22–23; ROMANS 12:20-21

PRAYER

Father, remind me when my anger rises against a person the enemy is using against me that they don't realize what they are really doing. Help me walk in love.

DECREE

I decree my love walk is on fire and burns up every agenda of the enemy to turn me into a vengeful person. I declare I walk in love even with those who hate me, in Jesus's name.

Examine Your Thoughts

*E*xamine your thoughts. Are you thinking like Me or are you thinking like your adversary, who roams about like a roaring lion seeking someone to devour? Are you thinking My thoughts, or are you meditating on the thoughts of fear, doubt, and unbelief the enemy is injecting into your soul? Are you aware of your thought life with all its machinations? As a man thinks in his heart, so is he. My thoughts are higher than your thoughts but the enemy's thoughts you take as your own will bring you low. Stop and think about what you are thinking about. The battle is in the mind, but the war is for your heart.

ISAIAH 55:8–9; JOSHUA 1:8; PROVERBS 23:7

PRAYER

Father, help me to think about what I am thinking about. Help me recognize the enemy's intrusion into my thought life immediately and reject his poisonous lies.

DECREE

I decree the enemy's thoughts are locked out of the sanctuary of my mind. I declare the meditations of my heart are pleasing in God's sight and torment the enemy, in Jesus's name.

The Enemy Is the Same Yesterday, Today, and Forever

I am your God. I am the same yesterday, today, and forever. The enemy of your soul is competing for godship in your life. He is also the same yesterday, today, and forever. Satan has no new tricks. He has no new strategies. He has no new tactics. He doesn't need any because mankind continues to fall for the tried-and-true lies. Rise up above your contemporaries who are so easily deceived by the lust of the flesh, the lust of the eyes, and the pride of life, and choose to serve Me with your whole heart. Stay close to Me and you will not fall for the devil's lies.

HEBREWS 13:8; JOHN 8:44; REVELATION 12:9

PRAYER

Father, help me discern the truth from a lie. Your Word is truth. Put me in remembrance of Your Word when the enemy is working to deceive me with crafty lies.

DECREE

I decree every enemy strategy and tactic is null and void in my life. I declare I discern every lie of the wicked one and reject it with everything in me, in Jesus's name.

Jesus Is the Stronger Man

Jesus rightly described your enemy as a strongman. But Jesus is the stronger man. Jesus is greater than any enemy stronghold and can deliver you from evil. Cry out to Me in His name and you will meet face to face with your deliverer. Jesus will empower you to overcome the strongman who has kept you in bondage. By way of the resurrection life and power that dwells inside of you, He will empower you to break free from every tie that binds you to death. The strongman may have you bound, but the stronger man in you will lead you into liberty.

MATTHEW 12:29; JOHN 10:10; PSALM 107:6

PRAYER

Father, thank You for delivering me from evil. Thank You for empowering me to overcome every strongman that works to kill, steal, and destroy my life.

DECREE

I decree every strongman holding my life hostage is discovered, bound, and cast out. I declare I am spoiling the strongman's house and taking back what he stole, in Jesus's name.

January 22

I Hear the Chatter against Your Mind

What worries you doesn't frustrate Me. What keeps you up at night doesn't keep Me up at night. What scares you and steals your peace does not move Me. Do you want to know why? Because I am not giving ear to the voice of the enemy. I hear his chatter against your mind, but it does not move Me. I see your end from your beginning. I created you in My image. I am standing with you, living inside of you, and leading and guiding you. Stop allowing the enemy to worry you, keep you up at night, scare you, and steal your peace. Walk with Me.

JOHN 16:33; 1 PETER 5:7; ISAIAH 9:6

PRAYER

Father, help me combat worry that plagues my mind when everything seems to be going wrong all at once. Teach me to walk in peace even when chaos surrounds me.

DECREE

I decree a divine reversal of the demonic chatter against my heart. I declare the voice of worry is silenced and I walk in the peace that passes all understanding, in Jesus's name.

January 23

Ask Me for the Word of Wisdom

I have all wisdom. I have the wisdom you need for every battle you will ever fight. I see the end from the beginning. I'm never blindsided by what blindsides you. Ask Me for a word of wisdom about the enemies plotting and planning against you. Have I not promised to show you things to come? Ask Me for a word of wisdom about the enemy's schemes against your church. Let Me use you to warn, sound the trumpet, and blow the alarm. Use this spiritual gift as a tactic in war.

1 CORINTHIANS 12:8; PROVERBS 4:6–7; JAMES 1:5

PRAYER

Father, I am asking for wisdom for the warfare I am facing now and the warfare that will come against me in the future. Give me a heads-up. Show me what the enemy is doing and how to overcome before the battle begins raging.

DECREE

I decree the wisdom of God I receive confounds the enemy of my soul in every battle. I declare the spiritual gifts inform my spiritual warfare and I am victorious, in Jesus's name.

Be Careful Who You Go to Battle With

When you go into battle, choose your fellow soldiers wisely. Do not take the foolish. Do not take the fearful. Do not take the presumptuous. Do not take those who are unskilled in battle. There is a time of training and a time of war. If you take people into war with you who are not properly prepared or who do not trust Me with their lives, you will open a door to the enemy in your camp and people will get hurt. You will have to expend your energy rescuing them from the snare of the fowler. You will bring more warfare on yourself. Be careful who you go to battle with.

JUDGES 7; LUKE 14:31; DEUTERONOMY 24:5

PRAYER

Father, give me wisdom to choose who I trust to war with me and send me people who are trustworthy to take into battle. Help me discern who really has my back.

DECREE

I decree demonic agendas are met with divine deployments on my behalf. I declare I am warring unto victory with few skilled warriors just like Gideon did, in Jesus's name.

Stop Fighting Every Battle Alone

Two are better than one. One can put a thousand to flight. Two can put ten thousand to flight. Yes, there are some battles you will have to fight alone. There are some enemies you will have to gain victory over in your own right by My authority and grace. But I have not called you to fight every battle alone. I have called you to go two by two into the enemy's camp like the lepers who sat at the gate. I have called you to be part of an army who goes in to battle the strongman and take the spoils. Stop fighting alone. Ask your brothers and sisters for the help you need to overtake the devil's plans for your life.

DEUTERONOMY 32:30; JOSHUA 23:10; LEVITICUS 26:8

PRAYER

Father, help me discern when I need reinforcements in the fight. Give me the grace of humility to understand I need help and the willingness to ask for the help I need, in Jesus's name.

DECREE

I decree a synergy in the spirit for warfare against the strongman. I declare victory beyond my wildest imagination is my portion in battle, in Jesus's name.

Don't Overreact to the Enemy's Maneuvers

*B*e careful not to overreact to the enemy's maneuvers. He's watching. He's examining you from top the bottom. He's exploring your reactions to his fiery darts. Will you rise up with the shield of faith and quench his onslaught? Or will you speak words of fear to your friends and family? Will you become anxious and overwhelmed? Or will you become bold as a lion in the face of the enemy's persecution against your life? Don't overreact. Stay calm. I am your peace. Look to Me, and I will help you stay the course to victory.

2 CORINTHIANS 12:9; PROVERBS 28; COLOSSIANS 3:15

PRAYER

Father, help me stay alert in the spirit so that I quickly recognize the enemy's presence. Put a guard over my mouth and draw me close to you when the enemy is raging against me.

DECREE

I decree a deluge of anxiety, pressure, and persecution against the enemy. I declare I walk in the Spirit and respond in the Spirit to every enemy onslaught, in Jesus's name.

Walk as Christ Walked the Earth

Selfishness opens the door to the devourer. Selflessness paves the way for me to move. When you act selfishly, you make poor decisions based on your needs and your needs alone. You end up in dangerous positions where the enemy can strike you because whatever is not of faith is sin. Selfishness is not of faith. When you walk in selflessness, you are walking as Christ walked in the earth. The enemy had no place in Him. He did not consider His own body or His own desires, but the desire of His heavenly Father who sent Him. Crucify self and slam the door on the enemy.

PHILIPPIANS 2:3–4; PROVERBS 19:17; GALATIANS 5:24

PRAYER

Father, help me to crucify my flesh. Give me the strength to pick up my cross and follow Jesus. Show me the bigger picture in the battle so I can get my mind off myself and on to others.

DECREE

I decree the devourer of my flesh is disallowed and disavowed. I declare temptations of the flesh are overcome by the force of my will to follow Jesus and I will overcome, in Jesus's name.

Beware the Lies in Your Eyes

*Y*our spiritual enemies and your foes are trying to bind you and blind you. Your wicked opponents are trying to throw lies in your eyes so you cannot discern the life I have for you. It's time to turn the tables. It's time to bind the enemy according to the authority the Father has given to you in the name of Jesus. It's time to blind the foes with the light of the Word. It's time to speak life and allow My Spirit to battle with and for you. Christ's words are spirit and life. Speak the Word of truth, light, and life and you will see clearly to bind your enemy and take back what he stole while you could not see him.

EPHESIANS 5:8; JOHN 1:5; MATTHEW 16:19

PRAYER

Father, open the eyes of my heart and help me see what I cannot see. Break off the blinders the enemy has erected around my vision so I can discern the lies rightly.

DECREE

I decree every demonic entity attacking my vision is bound. I declare my spiritual eyesight is clear, and I discern and resist the darkness that is working to overtake me, in Jesus's name.

January 29

Don't Bow to Any Other Spirit but Mine

Don't bow down to the ways of the world. Don't bow down to the imaginations of your heart. Continue to bow down to Me. Bow a knee to Me. Don't bow to the spirit of fear. Don't bow to that spirit of discouragement. I know it's tempting to give up and quit and run in the other direction. But don't do it! Run to Me. Run to the throne. Come boldly to My throne. My throne is a throne of grace. It's a throne of mercy. It's a throne where you can come at any moment, knowing that I will receive you, because you are in Christ.

PHILIPPIANS 2:9–11; PSALM 95:6; PSALM 5:7

PRAYER

Father, I bow down to You and You alone. You reign supreme in my life. Help me run to You and not away from You when the pressure from the spirit world feels overwhelming.

DECREE

I decree fear, discouragement, and imaginations bow to the Christ in me. I declare my heart bows to the Lord Jesus and to Him alone, in Jesus's name.

There's a Showdown Coming

I am making a way for you to come to that place of the showdown; to come to that place of overcoming; to come to that place where you will make the enemy bow, in Christ's name. I am ordering your steps to that place of encounter where you will see Jesus differently than you've ever seen Me before. You will see Jesus as the captain of the hosts. You will see Jesus as your provider in the midst of a famine. You will see Jesus as the One who loves your soul unconditionally and who will hold on to you through every storm and who will be there for you in every instance, whatever season you are walking in.

1 KINGS 18:20–40; PSALM 37:23; PSALM 54:4

PRAYER

Father, give me boldness to make the spiritual and natural confrontations I need to make to see Your will come to pass in my life. Help me lean on You completely.

DECREE

I decree the enemy quivers and flees when I am submitted to God and confront him with the blood of the Lamb. I declare storms dissipate and peace is my portion, in Jesus's name.

Meditate on My Promise of Provision

*B*eloved, I want you to be in health and prosper even as your soul prospers. So meditate on My promise of provision. When have you seen the righteous forsaken or My children begging bread? You are righteous in Christ. He is your righteousness, and your covenant with your heavenly Father includes provision. So, let your soul prosper by reading, meditating, studying, trusting, and believing what My Word says about your provision. I will not leave you begging bread.

PHILIPPIANS 4:19; PSALM 37:25; 3 JOHN 2

PRAYER

Father, I am grateful for my covenant with You. You are My provider. Help me not to waiver in my trust of Your ability and desire to take care of me and watch over me.

DECREE

I decree an overflow of Heaven's supply, Jehovah Jireh, the God of more than enough. I declare I am not a beggar—I am a king—and my needs are met, in Jesus's name.

FEBRUARY

Yet in all these things we are more than conquerors through Him who loved us. For I am persuaded that neither death nor life, nor angels nor principalities nor powers, nor things present nor things to come, nor height nor depth, nor any other created thing, shall be able to separate us from the love of God which is in Christ Jesus our Lord.

ROMANS 8:37–39

February 1

Your Redeemer Lives

*I*t is not My will for you to walk around with your head hung low. My will for you is to walk around with your head looking up because your redemption draws nigh. It comes from heavenly places. His name is Jesus. He redeemed you unto victory. I've not called you to walk around feeling sorry for yourself and wondering what bad thing might happen next. Evil forebodings are not your portion. So stop thinking about what might happen next to derail you. Stop thinking about all the bad things that could happen and begin to meditate on My goodness. Begin to meditate on My love.

LUKE 21:28; GALATIANS 3:3; PHILIPPIANS 4:6–7

PRAYER

Father, help me keep looking at my Redeemer, my justifier, and my victory banner. Help me catch You loving me. Draw me closer to You when the enemy is lurking.

DECREE

I decree my Redeemer lives and the enemy's plans to kill my blessing are bound. I declare God's goodness and favor surrounds me like a shield and I reign victorious in Christ, in Jesus's name.

When Darkness Threatens to Overtake You

*W*hen darkness threatens to overtake you, I will show you the way through what seems to be impenetrable darkness. I will show you the way out when you meditate on Me instead of the situation. I will order your steps when you meditate on My heart instead of the brokenness. When you meditate on that which I've told you in past seasons instead of that which the enemy is telling you right now, you will clearly see the path to victory. The darkness will flee. The shadows will give way to the illumination of My Word as you confess who you are and speak words of triumph.

JOSHUA 1:8; PSALM 1:2; PSALM 63:6

PRAYER

Father, remind me to meditate on Your Word day and night. Remind me to meditate on Your Word on my bed. Remind me to fix my eyes on You always.

DECREE

I decree my shining light weakens the enemy and overcomes threats of darkness. I declare the words of my mouth and the meditations of my heart are pleasing to the Lord, in Jesus's name.

February 3

You Will Have Opposition

*B*reakthrough and overcoming are concepts you like to walk in and realities I've provided for you. You are an overcomer, and I've called you to walk in a breakthrough lifestyle. But these concepts and realities point to another truth: you will have opposition. Jesus said in this world you will have tribulation. But He also said to be of good cheer because He has overcome the world. Your faith brings you into the victory that overcomes the world. Commit to continuously fighting the good fight of faith and you will walk in consistent breakthrough.

MICAH 2:13; JOHN 16:33; 1 JOHN 5:4

PRAYER

Father, thank You for being my breaker—my consistent breaker. Help me stay focused on Your victory instead of the trouble and follow Your lead as You break through.

DECREE

I decree breakthrough is my portion and I break through all opposition. I declare the enemy will not break me up or break me down, but I will break through in Christ, in Jesus's name.

Stop Confessing the Enemy's Lies

I hear My people confess rightly that the devil is a liar. Indeed, he is the father of lies and has been sinning from the beginning. You confess rightly. But you also confess his lies. My people repeat the deceitful whispers he speaks to their souls as if it's gospel truth. They dig in and take a stand on a lie clothed in fear. Confessing the devil is a liar is only lip service if you yield your mouth to the lies he whispers to your soul. Pay attention to your thought life. Catch the devil deploying his sneak attacks against your mind and cast his lies down quickly.

JOHN 8:44; HEBREWS 3:1; PSALM 19:14

PRAYER

Father, thank You for Your loving correction. Help me say about myself, my circumstances, my family, my finances—my life— what You are saying about me.

DECREE

I decree My mouth lines up with the Father of lights, not the father of lies. I declare my mouth shall not repeat the lies of the wicked one but the truth of the loving one, in Jesus's name.

My Love Will Help You Stand Strong

*W*hen the enemy wants you to look at his handiwork, choose to look at Me instead. It's not difficult to see what the enemy is doing—he comes to kill, steal, and destroy, and he leaves a trail behind him. It's more difficult to keep your eyes on Me in the midst of the mess the enemy has made. Do it anyway. Ask Me to help you stay focused on things above and not on the things of the world or the destruction of the enemy. Look at me again and again and again, until the image of My goodness is so stamped on your soul that nothing the enemy does can shake you from that stance. And remember, I will help you clean up the mess the enemy made.

PSALM 121:1–3; PSALM 105:4–11; PSALM 25:15

PRAYER

Father, help me see Your goodness in the midst of the rubble. Help me focus on Your redeeming power in the aftermath of a spiritual attack.

DECREE

I decree what the enemy meant for harm, God will turn for my good and His glory. I decree my eyes are fixed on the lover of my soul, the Lord Jesus Christ.

Determine to Take New Ground

$\mathcal{D}$on't be satisfied to just hold your place. Be determined to take new ground. Don't be satisfied to just merely keep maintaining your pace, but be determined to accelerate the Kingdom for My glory. Know and trust that I am able to help you take new ground. I am able to help you take new territories. I am able to help you see what you could not see in past seasons. I am able to help you move forward even when it feels like your ankles are broken, even when it feels like your knees are knocking, even when it feels like your muscles are so sore that you could not possibly move another step.

ISAIAH 40:31; HOSEA 10:12; JOSHUA 14:6–15

PRAYER

Father, stir my heart with determination to take the ground You want me to take. Strengthen me to be part of the increase of Your government in the earth.

DECREE

I decree everywhere my foot treads belongs to me as a steward in Christ's stead. I declare I possess a holy determination to occupy until Christ returns, in Jesus's name.

February 7

I Will Crush the Enemy's Plan

I will crush every enemy plan. I will crush every enemy attack. I will crush every insidious enemy onslaught against you when you keep your eyes on Me because I am the One who gives you the power to stand. I am the One who gives you the power to continue to walk through the fire. I am the One who gives you the power. So, stop looking at all the power of the enemy and how it has crushed you, how it has crushed your financial status, and how it has crushed your future. I have given you a hope and a future, and your future is not crushed.

PSALM 68:21; PSALM 91:13; ROMANS 16:20

PRAYER

Father, thank You for giving me power to crush the enemy's plans. Help me remember that the enemy's pressure and crushing cannot stand against the truth that sets me free.

DECREE

I decree the enemy of my future is crushed under Christ's feet. I declare I carry demon-crushing power in my mouth because of Christ's shed blood, in Jesus's name.

I Can Reverse the Curse

*Y*ou feel overwhelmed in your soul because of the witchcraft coming against your mind, because of the word curses coming against your life, because of the spiritual atmosphere in your home or your workplace—or sometimes just between your own ears. But I am able to reverse every word curse, hex, vex, spell, incantation, potion, evil decree—every expression of witchcraft. I am able to pick up the pieces, even if it's crushed into bits. So bind up the witchcraft and speak life when the power of death is harassing you. You will overcome.

GALATIANS 3:13; PROVERBS 26:2; 2 KINGS 9:22

PRAYER

Father, I break the power of being overwhelmed coming against my mind, and I push back witchcraft clouds from my midst. I break word curses, in Jesus's name.

DECREE

I decree the power of witchcraft cannot stand against the power that raised Christ from the dead that lives in me. I declare every curse released against me is broken, in Jesus's name.

I've Already Worked it Out

I know you cannot see beyond where you are right now because it looks as if your reality is your reality forever. Your present reality is not your future reality. Your present circumstances are not your future circumstances. I am the God of your future, and I have gone before you to clean up things that have happened in your past and things that are happening in your present. The enemy meant the attacks for harm, but I will make good come out of it. I've already worked it all out. Just trust Me. I've already worked it all out.

ROMANS 8:28; GENESIS 50:20; 1 PETER 2:18–20

PRAYER

Father, thank You for working all things out for my good. Help me wait on You to work it all the way out and not take matters into my own hands.

DECREE

I decree every enemy plan and plot against me will become a blessing in the end. I declare the God of my future has already made the crooked places straight for me, in Jesus's name.

When Things Begin to Shake, You Won't Shake

*W*hen you build upon Me, and when you walk upon Me and with Me and for Me, I am able to make the shaky places stable. I am able to make those parts of your soul, which in past seasons have caused you to self-sabotage, stable. You'll be able to walk and keep on walking. Even when things begin to shake, you won't shake. Even when things begin to rumble, and you feel like you're going to stumble, I am able to make you walk on an even keel. I am the One who will take your hand, and I will even put you on My back if I have to.

MATTHEW 7:24–27; PSALM 40:12–13; PSALM 16:8

PRAYER

Father, stabilize my soul when the enemy comes with lies that shake my faith. Help me stay steady so I won't stumble along the path You have called me to walk.

DECREE

I decree my feet are like hind's feet and I will not slip as I ascend to God's holy mountain. I declare that my mind is fixed, my heart is surrendered to God, in Jesus's name.

I Will Send Reinforcements

*C*ontinue plowing. Continue pushing. Continue pressing. Don't stop because things don't look right. Don't stop because people around you come against you. Don't stop because you can't see the end from the beginning, because I see it. I know the path. I am the way through the warfare to the victory. Don't you think I'm with you? Don't you think I'll tell you what you need to know? Don't you think I'll send you the reinforcements?

1 CORINTHIANS 10:13; 2 CORINTHIANS 4:18; PSALM 20:2–9

PRAYER

Father, give me a persevering heart so I can keep on pressing, plowing, and pushing through the resistance to Your will in my life. Send reinforcements quickly.

DECREE

I decree the enemy's reinforcements are fainting. I declare angels are on assignment to back me up and help me through the warfare that is raging against my life, in Jesus's name.

Don't Fear My Will

*F*ear will work like a thief in your life. But it's not just about a fear of speaking or a fear of rejection or a fear of vulnerability that keeps you distant from those I've called you to connect with. It's often the fear of My perfect will that holds you back. Don't be afraid of My will. Don't be afraid of what I've called you to. Don't be afraid of the devils along the path, because I am your Lord and I am greater than these things. Don't let the spirit of fear talk you out of your destiny. War against fear.

JOSHUA 1:9; PSALM 56:3; PSALM 23:4

PRAYER

Father, help me to discern fear in all its subtle manifestations. Give me a boldness and a confidence that supersedes the lies fear shouts at my soul.

DECREE

I decree fear is powerless to hold me back from God's good, perfect, and acceptable will for my life. I declare war on the enemy named fear and all its cousins, in Jesus's name.

Bounce Back from a Lack Attack

When you suffer a lack attack, you can quickly bounce back by renewing your mind to My Word. There is no lack manifesting in your life from which the truth cannot set you free. The truth is everything you put your hand to will prosper. The truth is I will supply all your needs according to Christ's riches in glory. The truth is I have given you the power to create wealth. Don't meditate on the lack or the attack. Meditate on My provision and receive.

PSALM 34:10; JAMES 1:4; PSALM 23:1

PRAYER

Father, help me rest in You as Jehovah Jireh. I stand in faith with a hand that sows and a heart that receives Your abundant provision in my life.

DECREE

I decree provision chases me down and overtakes me in every godly venture and in every fundamental need in my life. I declare the lack attack against me is broken, in Jesus's name.

February 14

Love Battles for You

There is a war against your mind concerning the revelation of My love. You know in part and you have experienced it in part. You see in part, and you are longing for more of My love, even though you don't know it. The enemy has done all he can—he has pulled out all the stops—to keep you busy and striving and warring for what I have already given to you. Stop. Take a deep breath. Understand and know that I love you. I really love you. I went to war for you, and I keep battling for you. I am with you. I'm calling you today into a new level, a new measure of trust, a new level of abandonment, a new level of surrender, and a new level of glory.

1 CORINTHIANS 13:4–7; JOHN 3:16; ROMANS 5:8

PRAYER

Father, give me a greater revelation of Your love for me. Help me to really receive Your love so I can war from a position of knowing that You will never leave me.

DECREE

I decree I am loved and accepted in the beloved. I declare I walk in love and in a revelation of the power of love to overcome the hate of the wicked one, in Jesus's name.

February 15

See the Light

$\mathscr{I}$am your healer, and I am your deliverer. So don't look around and about and see the darkness. Look around and about and see the light. For I am your expectation and your hope. I am the One who causes you to walk in victory. I am the One who has seated you far above all principalities and powers. You are seated in a position of rulership and you have authority over the works of darkness. Don't come up under them but begin to resist them. Speak out against them. Sound the alarm and let all those around and about you know you have won the victory.

EPHESIANS 2:6; EPHESIANS 1:19–21; 1 JOHN 3:8

PRAYER

Father, remind me of where I really stand—and sit—in the spirit realm. Holy Spirit, put me in remembrance of who I really am and the victory that belongs to me. Help me see rightly.

DECREE

I decree that the light in me overtakes the darkness around and about me. I declare I am healed, delivered, and walk in total freedom in Christ as I resist the wicked one, in Jesus's name.

February 16

Oil Your Shield

The days of warfare as usual are over. I am calling you to oil your shield and lift up your sword in a new way. The tactics that worked in the past will not work in the battles ahead. The new way is love. The new way is humility. Too many have taken pride in their spiritual warfare skills, which causes Me to resist them in the heat of the battle because apart from Me they can do nothing. War by walking in love. War by walking in My Word. Beyond this, I will show you new strategies for every individual skirmish. Lean on Me.

ISAIAH 21:5; JAMES 4:6; PROVERBS 5:3–6

PRAYER

Father, teach me the new tactics and the new strategies for war. Help me walk in love and humility as I lift up my shield and swing my sword. You alone are the source of my victory.

DECREE

I decree my shield is only because I am intimate with the Holy Spirit. I declare I walk on the cutting edge of new revelation to win the battle, in Jesus's name.

February 17

Beware of Beating the Air

Stop beating the air. Stop presuming to know what is going on in the spirit without prayer. If you ask Me, I will show you the source of your opposition when it benefits you to know. If you pray, I will reveal to you the root of the warfare you need to see. When you assume and presume, you are often stirring up more spiritual fights against you. So stop and ask Me. I know what you are up against, and I will show you what you need to see in the moment. You will walk in victory.

1 CORINTHIANS 9:26; LUKE 3:9; HEBREWS 5:14

PRAYER

Father, warn me when I am walking in assumption and presumption about the enemy. Give me greater discernment so that I can see the root of the warfare and lay an axe to it.

DECREE

I decree the enemy's attempts to put me off track misfire. I declare every hidden demon power is exposed by the insight of Christ, in Jesus's name.

Don't Take On Any and Every Battle

*N*ot every battle is yours to fight. Though I will call you to stand in the gap and make up the hedge, though I will call you to self-sacrificial intercessory warfare at times, you must discern the green light in the spirit before stepping on to the battlefield. You must recognize the unction in your heart to move into position to take the enemy down. Don't go unless I send you. I will always lead you into triumph, but you have to follow Me. Wait on my signal.

2 SAMUEL 15:9; 2 CORINTHIANS 2:14

PRAYER

Father, help me remember to ask You, "Shall I go up?" before running to the battle line. Help me not to leave You out of the spiritual warfare equation. Lead me.

DECREE

I decree the enemy's efforts to distract me with unnecessary fights are wrecked. I declare soulish compassion does not lead me into the wrong battles, in Jesus's name.

Raise Up a Battle Cry

Cry aloud! Cry all the more. Let your voice be heard. Raise your voice up with a battle cry. Don't be silent in this hour, in this hour of the attack, in this time of war, in this season of taking it all back. But see and know that I am with you and I will help you recover all. You've got to lift up your voice with a declaration of war—a clear sound and a clear signal to the mighty men, to the warriors—that it is time to advance. It is time to go up. It is time to follow Me into battle to take back what the enemy stole, to take back your peace of mind, to take back your family, and to take back your finances.

JOEL 2:1; JOEL 3:9; PSALM 142:1

PRAYER

Father, hear me when I cry. Acknowledge my declaration of war and send angels to fight with and for me. Empower me to take back what the devil stole.

DECREE

I decree my voice shakes hell. I declare that my battle cry will assemble the intercessors in formation, and we will send the devil packing and take back the spoils, in Jesus's name.

Keep Getting Back Up

I don't expect you to be perfect. When you fall, get back up again. Even when you've made the same mistake one thousand times, if you continue to declare war on your wrong behavior, you will eventually gain victory over bad habits. One way to define spiritual warfare is simply "outlasting the devil." So when you sin, repent. If you sin again, repent again. Just keep getting back up. A righteous man falls seven times and gets back up again. Don't stop warring against the sin that's warring against you. I will give you the strength to stand against anything and everything that is standing against you—even your flesh. Lean into Me when you feel weak.

ISAIAH 41:10; MARK 10:27; PROVERBS 24:16

PRAYER

Father, strengthen me in my weak areas. Give me a persevering spirit to press past my flesh and the temptations of the enemy and stand in Christ's righteousness.

DECREE

I decree that the spirit of fainting faints in my daunting presence. I declare I am growing in grace and I am being changed from glory to glory and strength to strength, in Jesus's name.

Force the Devil Out

The devil has forced his way into some of your circumstances, but now it's time to force him out, in the name of Jesus! He came in while you weren't looking. He sowed tares in your field while you were sleeping. He forced his way in while you were hurting. He moved in while you were too tired to notice. But I say to you, the Kingdom of God suffers violence and the violent take it by force. You've suffered violence at the enemy's forceful hand. Now get forceful in your authority over his wicked works and take back what belongs to you.

MARK 3:27; MATTHEW 11:12; MATTHEW 13:24-30

PRAYER

Father, help me discern where the enemy has made inroads into any area of my life so I can force him out. Help me rise up with courage and cast him out.

DECREE

I decree the devil is evicted from my premises, my mind, my health, my family, and my finances. I declare my violent faith overcomes the wicked one, in Jesus's name.

Laugh At Your Enemies

*W*hen you look at your spiritual enemies through My eyes, you'll laugh like I laugh. I smile over you, because you are My beloved one. I sing over you with songs of deliverance. But I am not smiling down on the demons who are opposing you. I am laughing heartily because I see their end. If you could just see the outcome. If you could just focus on Christ, your victory banner. If you could just see from My perspective, you would also laugh at your enemies. You can't lose in Christ. Keep smiling. Keep singing. Keep laughing.

PSALM 37:13; PSALM 2:4; PHILIPPIANS 4:4

PRAYER

Father, help me see the enemies of my soul through Your eyes of love. Help me see the end from the beginning—the victory enforced—and Your will done in my life.

DECREE

I decree my season of mourning is over and my triumph is here. I declare that as my heavenly Father laughs, I will laugh, sing, shout my praises, and do a victory dance, in Jesus's name.

I Call You Blessed

Some people call you betrayed, but I call you blessed. Some call you defeated, but I call you blessed. Some call you overwhelmed, but I call you blessed. Whatever circumstances you find yourself in, remember this: your circumstances can be circumvented through prayer. Cry out to Me. I am the God who blesses you in the presence of your enemies. I am the God who overwhelms your enemies with confusion when you call upon My name in faith. You are blessed.

PROVERBS 3:33; PSALM 21:3; PSALM 21:6

PRAYER

Father, I rejoice in Your blessing because with Your hand of power on my life, I cannot fail. Remind me that no matter what the enemy calls me, You call me blessed and so I am blessed.

DECREE

I decree the enemy of my blessing is burned with double fire. I declare I am blessed beyond measure with every spiritual blessing in heavenly places, in Jesus's name.

I Will Give You Every Place Your Foot Treads

Keep advancing. Don't slow down now. Keep pushing forward. Keep forging ahead. Keep your eyes on Me as you move onward. I am giving you every place where your foot treads. Yes, you will face giants. Yes, you will face haters. Yes, you will face your own flesh. Yes, your weary soul may want to give up on the edge of breakthrough. But now is not the time to pull back. Now is the time to pull forward. You will win if you don't quit.

DEUTERONOMY 11:24; JOSHUA 1:3; ROMANS 10:5

PRAYER

Father, by Your word I can run through a troop and leap over a wall. Thank You for strengthening me against the opposition working to weary me and giants that intimidate me.

DECREE

I decree my haters and my foes will stumble and fall when they rise up against me. I declare I am steadily advancing the government of God in the earth, in Jesus's name.

I Will Give You a Glimpse

*M*ount up with wings like eagles. You will gain new strength. You will run your race with new vigor. Come away with Me. Come up higher and begin to see through My eyes. For My ways are higher than your ways, and My thoughts are higher than your thoughts, but I will give you a glimpse. I will show you things to come, and I will warn you of the enemy attacks, and I will encircle you with My angels because I love you.

Isaiah 40:31; Isaiah 55:8–9; Psalm 34:7

PRAYER

Father, thank You for opening my eyes so I can gain a new perspective in this battle. Help me think like You think, see like You see, and war like You war unto victory.

DECREE

I decree the enemy cannot hide from my discerning eyes but is found out and cast out. I declare my eyes see the goodness of God and the victory He has attained for me, in Jesus's name.

When You Are Your Own Worst Enemy

The enemy of your soul is absolutely real, but many times you serve as your own worst enemy. You allow your emotions to rule and reign instead of following the leadership of My Spirit. You allow your opinions to inform your will rather than My Word. You allow the enemy to manipulate you with whispers you don't cast down. Be vigilant and sober-minded. Pay attention to your thoughts and the intentions of your heart. Submit what you think, what you feel, and what you want to My Spirit.

PROVERBS 25:28; PSALM 26:2; LUKE 22:42

PRAYER

Father, I surrender my will to Your will. I surrender my emotions to Your Word. I surrender my opinions to Your way. Help me be alert to self-sabotage.

DECREE

I decree the enemy's mind manipulation is melted by God's cleansing fire. I declare I walk in discipline and self-control and there is no room for the enemy in my mind, in Jesus's name.

February 27

You Will See Justice in Your Life

You will see justice on all sides as you press into the understanding of who I really am. I am your justifier. I am the God that makes the wrong things right, the crooked places straight. I am the One who works all things together for your good. So, trust Me and love Me and walk with Me and seek My face, not just My hand. Seek My heart, not just My provision. All these things will be added to you as you seek Me and My Kingdom.

AMOS 5:24; ISAIAH 30:18; PSALM 33:5

PRAYER

Father, strengthen me to wait on Your justice. Help me focus on You as my justifier and to trust You as the just judge who sees all things and makes all things right for those He loves.

DECREE

I decree justice is my portion and it shall satisfy my soul in due time. I declare my steadfast faith in God as the lawgiver, judge, and jury in my life, in Jesus's name.

Press Into Discernment

$\mathcal{M}$any want to grow in the gift of prophecy or grow in the gift of miracle-working. I am always pleased to see My people desire spiritual gifts. Fewer, though, press into the gift of discerning of spirits. This gift is vital in the days in which you live and the days that approach because many false ones will arise, and the darkness, great darkness, will begin to settle on the land. Many will be deceived because they do not discern. Practice discernment now, and earnestly desire My gifts.

PHILIPPIANS 1:9–10; HEBREWS 4:12; 1 KINGS 3:9

PRAYER

Father, just as King Solomon did, I am asking You for discernment to judge between good and evil. Grant me this request so I can avoid the coming deception.

DECREE

I decree a divine exchange in my life—deception for discernment. I declare I discern every demonic attack that works to move me away from the truth, in Jesus's name.

Eat the Bread of Life

Deliverance is the children's bread, but My children have to want the freedom My Son died to give them. When I confront something in your heart, when I put My finger on an issue in your soul, don't resist Me. Eat the bread of life and escape the snares of the enemy's trap. Your adversary will use what is in you and feed up on it to bring death to your joy, mourning to your dancing, and misery to your soul. Eat the bread of deliverance and fight your opponent with My weapons.

MATTHEW 4:4; PSALM 34:7; PSALM 34:4

PRAYER

Father, I welcome the confrontation and conviction of Your Spirit. Show me where I've gone wrong. Deliver me from evil thoughts and deeds so I can avoid the enemy's snare.

DECREE

I decree I am delivered and set free from every tie that binds my body and soul. I declare I feast on the bread of life, and I am quick to repent when I miss the mark, in Jesus's name.

MARCH

So David rose early in the morning, left the sheep with a keeper, and took the things and went as Jesse had commanded him. And he came to the camp as the army was going out to the fight and shouting for the battle. For Israel and the Philistines had drawn up in battle array, army against army. And David left his supplies in the hand of the supply keeper, ran to the army, and came and greeted his brothers.

1 SAMUEL 17:20–22

Thank Me in Advance

Thank Me in advance of your victory because the truth is your victory was secured at Calvary. Thank Me in advance of the breakthrough because the truth is Jesus is your breaker and He has already broken through your opposition. Thank Me for the grace to continue to stand and withstand in the evil day because I am able to make you stand against every wicked foe. Thank Me because when you do, you shift your focus to the outcome I want for you instead of the outcome the enemy has planned for you.

PSALM 103:2; 1 THESSALONIANS 5:18; EPHESIANS 5:20

PRAYER

Father, I thank You for the grace to stand against the wicked one. Help me walk in a spirit of thanksgiving and focus on Your power when I feel too weak to utter Your name.

DECREE

I decree the sound of thanksgiving from my heart pierces the enemy's ears. I declare my heart is grateful because the breakthrough is assured and the outcome is triumph, in Jesus's name.

March 2

Don't Fear the Nocturnal Warfare

Nocturnal warfare may rage against you, but Psalm 91 stands true for you. You don't have to be afraid of the terror by night or the dark pestilence that invades in the midnight hours. I have promised My beloved sweet rest, and when you trust in Me, I will bring you peace while you slumber. I have given you authority over nocturnal warfare. I have given you My angels to watch over you. You can lay your head down at night with confidence. Do not be afraid.

PROVERBS 3:24; PSALM 91; 2 TIMOTHY 1:7

PRAYER

Father, I take authority now over nocturnal warfare. Give me sweet sleep. Surround me with angels to protect me in the midnight hour. Shut out enemy attacks.

DECREE

I decree Psalm 91 over my life, my family, my finances, and everything that pertains to me. I declare that nocturnal warfare cannot stand in the light of the gospel, in Jesus's name.

I Am Guaranteeing Your Payback

When you seek Me, there's a guaranteed provision; there's a guaranteed healing; there's a guaranteed redemption; there's a guaranteed payback from your losses. When you seek Me with all your heart, you will find Me. So begin to seek Me even now, in a fresh way, in a new way, in a deeper way. Lay aside all the distractions that come to nip at your heels, that cause you to want to look down, look to the right, look to the left, or look behind you. Look up, for your redemption draws nigh. Look up, for this is where you will see My glory. Look up, for this is where you will receive from My Spirit, with your hands raised and your heart open wide.

JEREMIAH 29:13; LUKE 21:28; HEBREWS 12:1

PRAYER

Father, I aim to lift my head and my hands and my heart to You. Help me stay focused so I can receive everything You have for me by faith.

DECREE

I decree the enemy working to shatter my wholeness is shattered. I declare my heart shall not waiver and my head shall not bow down, but I will look to my source, in Jesus's name.

When Spiritual Witchcraft Attacks

The spirit of witchcraft may attack you, but don't bow to it. Don't run into a cave and hide with the demonic imaginations attacking your mind. Don't repeat Elijah's mistake in running away from Jezebel after a great triumph. Know your enemy. Do not be ignorant of his devices. But know me, the God of your victory. Stand and face the attack head-on, and you will cast down witchcraft's swirl against your life. You will not fall.

1 KINGS 19:2–3; 1 KINGS 19:9; 2 KINGS 9:22

PRAYER

Father, I bow to Christ and Christ alone, but the temptation to bow to the warfare is real. Strengthen me to stand against every weapon that tries to prosper against me.

DECREE

I decree the glory of God insulates me from Jezebel's witchcraft. I declare witchcraft bounces off me and returns to the sender in the second Heaven, in Jesus's name.

Protection from Creeping Demons

*W*hen you see me as your shield you will not shrink back from the battle. I am faithful to protect you. I am faithful to shelter you under My shadow, where no foe can stand. I am a warrior. The Lord is My name. When you walk with Me, you are protected from the creeping demons that seek to ensnare you. I will whisper to your heart directions and strategies to avoid every snare. See Me as your shield and let me use you as My battle axe.

PSALM 18:2; PSALM 91:3-4

PRAYER

Father, shield me from the arrows and flaming missiles the evil one throws my way. Show me which way to go to avoid the traps the enemy has put in my path.

DECREE

I decree chaos to the creeping demons. I declare the shadow of His wings keeps me safe from the fiery darts that come faster than I can lift my shield of faith, in Jesus's name.

When Your Enemies Look Like Family

Sometimes your enemies look just like people you know. Sometimes they look like your closest friends or your family. Remember, people are not your enemy, but the enemy does use people to hurt you. Move in the opposite spirit of the demonic agenda that's moving against you. Decide to act like My Son, to walk the extra mile, to turn the other cheek, and to speak to the spirits tempting you not to trust Me for your deliverance.

ROMANS 12:17–21; 1 PETER 3:9; MATTHEW 5:38–48

PRAYER

Father, help me separate the principality from the personality. Help me rightly divide between the flesh and the devil, and grace me to return good for evil.

DECREE

I decree provoking spirits working to get a rise out of me are paralyzed. I declare when demon-inspired and flesh-driven people come against me, I will walk in love, in Jesus's name.

March 7

There Is Safety in My Presence

I will lift you up. I will preserve you. I will invite you into My remnant. And you will see and know that there is safety in My presence. And you will not have to worry; you do not have to fear. So, do your part because I've done My part. I've kept My promises to you, now keep your vows to Me. Don't put off any longer doing those things which I told you to do because of the war that rages against you. I am with you.

2 THESSALONIANS 3:3; DEUTERONOMY 31:6; ISAIAH 41:10

PRAYER

Father, remind me to run into Your preserving presence when I discern the attack against my life. Help me not to procrastinate or put off coming to Your throne.

DECREE

I decree my enemies are thwarted in the presence of the one true living God. I declare My God is waiting for me, to rescue and protect me from the enemy's fiery darts, in Jesus's name.

I Will Make You Soar Again

I am able to make you move again. I am able to make you soar again. I am able to make you go forth with breakneck speed again even in the midst of the enemy attack. So stop being satisfied with standing and withstanding and start hungering and thirsting to advance My Kingdom at an even greater pace in the midst of the warfare so you can show the enemy that My grace is sufficient and show the naysayers around you that there truly is a call upon your life, that you might show forth My grace and My praises even in the midst of the battle.

ISAIAH 40:31; EXODUS 19:4; MATTHEW 5:6

PRAYER

Father, let Your wind blow at my back so I can run faster, soar higher, and move beyond the enemy attack. Vindicate me from the wagging tongues that speak against me.

DECREE

I decree every naysayer who is speaking against my life will be shown to be in the wrong. I declare I live, move, and have my being in the Lord of hosts, in Jesus's name.

Determine to Drive Out the Enemy

*N*ow is the time to be determined to take new ground, to advance the Kingdom, to attack old enemies who come around cyclically. Now is the time to make another push. Now is the time to get determined and redetermined. It's time to re-up! Let go of the resentment and let go of the bitterness that can come with prolonged warfare. Let go of the weariness. Let them go. Put them in My capable hands, and let Me throw them back in the enemy's face because I work all things together for good.

2 CHRONICLES 20:17; PHILIPPIANS 4:13; EPHESIANS 4:31

PRAYER

Father, renew in me a determined heart that rises up despite the ongoing battles. Help me to let go of the weariness, the bitterness, and the malice that plagues my soul.

DECREE

I decree a rapid return of everything the enemy stole with interest. I declare I am walking out of the bitterness of war with a better Kingdom perspective, in Jesus's name.

The Enemy Attack Will Bounce Off You

That which the enemy used to try to destroy you will rebound off you and land back in his dark camp, and there will be confusion, but not for you. I am bringing you out of that place of confusion and into a place of knowing, into a place of confidence that you hear My voice, into a place of understanding what My will is. You can do all things through Christ who strengthens you. That needs to be your confession. Look at Me. And look again and again and again until the image of My goodness is so stamped on your soul that nothing the enemy does can shake you from that stance.

JOHN 10:27–28; PSALM 123:1; PSALM 100:5

PRAYER

Father, bring clarity to my mind and peace to my heart when the enemy attacks me. Cause the fiery targets to rebound off me and return to the wicked one's camp.

DECREE

I decree no weapon formed against me shall prosper. I declare every tongue that rises up against me shall be condemned and the curse causeless shall not land, in Jesus's name.

Demon Powers Run in Packs

*Y*our spiritual enemies run in packs. They tag team against in you in the spiritual wrestling match, bringing the right opponent against you at what looks like the most opportune time. But you have the ultimate tag team on your side—Father, Son, and Holy Spirit. And you have the angels fighting for you. Know that the enemy works coordinated attacks against you. But know that I have coordinated your victory long before the battle was even won.

EPHESIANS 6:12; ROMANS 8:31; LUKE 4:10

PRAYER

Father, help me be swift to see the packs of demons coming my way so I can assemble prayer warriors to stand and withstand with me. Release the warring angels on my behalf.

DECREE

I decree every coordinated attack orchestrated against me is laid waste. I declare my counterattack overwhelms the packs of demons swarming around me, in Jesus's name.

The War Against Battle Weariness

I know you feel weary in the warfare, but you don't have to stay that way. I have told you in My Word that the enemy comes to weary the saints, and I have told you not to grow weary. When you are weary, it's a sign you did not turn to Me fast enough to help you carry the burden and fight the battle. But it's not too late. I am a very present help in time of need. You can run and not grow weary when you wait on Me. I am waiting on you. Come to Me.

DANIEL 7:25; GALATIANS 6:9; PSALM 55:22

PRAYER

Father, give me the grace to stand against the assignment of weariness that works to discourage my heart and weaken my hands. Draw me close to You, and don't let go.

DECREE

I decree weariness bows now to the resurrection power that lives inside me. I declare I am energized, and as I fight my spiritual foes, I get more energized, in Jesus's name.

It's a Fixed Fight

*I*t may look like there is a battle between light and darkness in the world, in your life, or even in your mind. But it's a fixed fight. If you will stand in the light, you will walk in freedom. If you will stand in the light, you will see the enemy's lies for what they are. If you will stand in the light, you will see yourself the way I see you. Darkness cannot overcome the light. My light is in You, and you are in My light. Open your eyes and watch the darkness flee.

MATTHEW 5:14–16; 1 PETER 2:9; JOHN 1:5

PRAYER

Father, lead me and guide me into Your light when I start approaching dark places. Open my eyes so I can see where I am going. Teach me how to watch and pray.

DECREE

I decree darkness that opposes me will submit to the light in me. I declare darkness trembles in my presence because the living God dwells within me, in Jesus's name.

When Ancient Spirits Attack You

*A*ncient spirits may attack you, but I am the Ancient of Days. I am the Creator of the universe. I created thrones and principalities and dominions and principalities and powers. I created everything that exists. Ancient spirits have no more authority over you because you are in Me and I am in you. So know that ancestral spirits and ancient spirits must bow to the Ancient of Days on the inside of you. I have prepared you for victory eternal. Eternity past and the spirits that dwelled there have no power over you.

DANIEL 7:9–10; COLOSSIANS 1:6; EPHESIANS 1:21

PRAYER

Father, I come to your throne of grace boldly, and from that position I dethrone every enemy power working to control my soul and sway my flesh.

DECREE

I decree ancient spirits must bow to the Ancient of Days. I declare my Creator God did not create me for defeat at the hand of the enemy but for consistent triumph, in Jesus's name.

Reject Offense that Leads to Deception

I was betrayed and continue to be betrayed every day by believers who fall away from My heart. I am the rock of offense, and many grow offended with Me because things in their life don't work out the way they had hoped. In the last days, many will be offended, and that offense leads to deception. Many who are offended with you and have betrayed you have merely fallen to the temptation of deception based on smoke and mirrors. I understand the pain of betrayal. I will never betray you. Come to Me for healing.

JEREMIAH 17:14; PSALM 34:17–20; PSALM 147:3

PRAYER

Father, guard me from the spirit of offense. Endue me with the grace of forgiveness so I can act like You. Keep me from the temptation to shut down when people betray me.

DECREE

I decree a gag order on the voice of offense speaking into my life. I declare that when betrayal comes, I will choose to turn the other cheek and pray, in Jesus's name.

Use the Adversity to Your Advantage

Adversity is to your ultimate advantage. Adversity will not kill you. Adversity will make you stronger. Adversity will make you wiser. Adversity will leave you with more compassion for others who are enduring struggles and suffering in life. See adversity as an opportunity and not an end-all. The adversity will not last forever, but the lessons you learn contending with your adversary the devil will prepare you for greater victories in the days ahead.

2 Chronicles 15:7; Psalm 34:19; Psalm 118:5–6

PRAYER

Father, You created me for adversity, and I was born for war. Help me keep the right perspective when adversity and opposition threaten to derail me.

DECREE

I decree the adversary of my soul is restrained and restricted from bringing destruction in my life. I declare adversity makes me stronger and spurs me to fight harder, in Jesus's name.

Take Authority Over Your Finances

*R*ise up in the authority I have given you to create wealth, and witty inventions will come unto you. Begin to sow where I tell you to sow, and you'll see a harvest because I have appointed a harvest for you. I have released angels of abundant harvest to help you bring it in, but you must be obedient to give. You must be obedient to sow. You must be obedient to do what I've told you to do in My Word and then you can take full authority over every attack against the provision I've promised.

PROVERBS 8:2; 2 CORINTHIANS 9:10; DEUTERONOMY 18:1–14

PRAYER

Father, lead me and guide me to sow in the ground You have designated for me. Show me where to plant my seed, how much to plant, and teach me how to reap the harvest.

DECREE

I decree I have the power to create wealth to establish God's covenant in the earth. I declare abundance is my portion and my harvest is perpetual, in Jesus's name.

Don't Let the Enemy Distract You

*Y*ou have been distracted. You have looked to a place that I have not called you to look. You've been looking for contentment in places I have not called you to. You've been looking for blessings in places I have not ordained for you. Begin to look at me. Gaze at My beauty and tune out all the other voices that come to distract you. Tune out all the imaginations that come at your soul. Incline your ear to Me, even for a moment, and I will show you things to come. I will give you clarity on even the decisions you have to make in the days ahead. I will give you understanding of some of the things that are going on.

1 CORINTHIANS 14:10; PSALM 27:4; PROVERBS 16:3

PRAYER

Father, help me stay in lockstep with Your heart and refuse to allow the enemy to fool me into looking to the right to the left. Give me peace, clarity, and understanding.

DECREE

I decree every demonic voice speaking to me falls on deaf ears, but God's voice lands on attentive ears. I declare I walk in supernatural wisdom and understanding, in Jesus's name.

Be a Believing Warrior

*B*e a believing believer—a believing warrior. For many are not walking in belief in the face of enemy opposition, but they are walking in bewilderment. When the enemy brings a trial to their doorstep, they think it strange. They question Me. They wonder if I love them any longer. No matter what the enemy throws your way, keep believing that I am good. Keep believing that I am your Deliverer. Keep believing I have a way of escape for you, just like David in the wilderness running from Saul. Many will be your spiritual enemies, but if you only believe and reject bewilderment you will overcome the enemy at every turn.

1 Peter 4:12–13; Psalm 23:6; 2 Samuel 22:2–4

PRAYER

Help me, Lord, to see you as my Deliverer, who brings me through the way of escape in every trial. Help me remember that You are a good, good Father.

DECREE

I decree bewilderment, confusion, worry, and fear have no place in my life. I declare my confidence in the Lord God Almighty who delivers me from every enemy, in Jesus's name.

Break Word Curses Against You

𝒫eople may curse you, but I call you blessed. The curse causeless shall not land if you don't let it. Remember who you are and your Kingdom rights. You are redeemed from the curse of the law. Jesus Christ was made a curse for you. Don't wait to feel the effects of word curses—the power of death in the tongues of your enemies—to land on you. Take initiative and take authority and break and bind curses released against you when you sense them in the spirit. People may curse you, but I have blessed you with every spiritual blessing.

GALATIANS 3:13; PSALM 26:2; ISAIAH 54:17

PRAYER

Father, I bless those who curse me and pray for those who use me. Forgive them for operating in jealously, hatred, or competition, and help me rise above the fray.

DECREE

I decree every curse that is launched against me is reversed and returned to the demon power that inspired it. I declare curses cannot land on my life because I am blessed, in Jesus's name.

Know Your Real Enemy

The enemy is behind your hurt and your pain. He uses people to slash you. He uses spirits to release voices of condemnation against you. He uses your unrenewed mind against you at every turn. It's time for you to rise up and get mad at the real enemy—not the people who he used, but the spirits that operate to keep you in bondage to the pain of the past, the angst of the present, and the fear of the future. Know your enemy and know that My Word contains the power to renew your mind to the truth that sets you free.

ROMANS 12:2; HEBREWS 4:12; EPHESIANS 4:26–27

PRAYER

Father, help me see the root of the warfare and resist the temptation to point fingers at people for my pain and suffering. Help me turn my anger toward the real enemy of my soul.

DECREE

I decree every enemy that has my destruction in mind will fall into his own trap. I declare I am free from the pain and suffering the enemy inflicted upon me in the last season, in Jesus's name.

My Shield of Faith Is Not Heavy

I see your weariness. I see your attempts to hold up your shield of faith even when you are carrying the weight of the world on your shoulders. Let me give you some wisdom: If you cast your cares on Me, you'll be in a much better position to hold up your shield of faith. For the cares of this world weigh you down and make everything seem heavier than it really is. My shield of faith is not heavy. You are able to hold it up and quench the fiery darts of the enemy when you let go of the cares I've not called you to carry.

PROVERBS 12:25; EPHESIANS 6:16; MARK 4:19

PRAYER

Father, I cast my cares on You. Take my worries and my weariness, and give me peace and strength to stand against the wiles of the wicked one. I surrender all to You.

DECREE

I decree every enemy that is working overtime to weary my soul is worn out and gives up. I declare my good, good Father is working everything out for my good, in Jesus's name.

Look for Opportunities to Break Yokes

Father anointed Jesus of Nazareth to go around doing good and to heal all who are oppressed of the enemy. He's anointed you to continue the work of Christ on the earth. The anointing on your life will break the yoke the enemy has put around the necks of others. So look around you and find the opportunities to use the yoke-breaking anointing Father has put on your life to see captives set free. Do the work of Christ and destroy the works of darkness.

ISAIAH 10:27; ISAIAH 9:4–7; 1 JOHN 3:8

PRAYER

Father, thank You for your anointing to serve in the Kingdom. Show me opportunities to set captives free with the anointing of the Holy Spirit and the name of Jesus.

DECREE

I decree every yoke the enemy has laid upon my neck is broken now. I declare the anointing on my life breaks every bondage off the people to whom God sends me, in Jesus's name.

Test the Spirits

*B*eloved, test the spirits. Deception is rising rapidly in this hour. Part of your spiritual warfare is warring against the deception of the day. Guard your mind. Guard your heart with all diligence for out of it flow the issues of life. Test the spirits that are speaking to you against My Word. Don't follow after every wind of doctrine that emerges in the church. Don't follow after every prophetic word spoken over your life. Test the spirits because the darkness is rising. Walk in the light.

1 John 4:1; Ephesians 5:6; 2 Thessalonians 2:3

PRAYER

Father, give me a spiritual awareness to detect the spirit behind the words people speak and the spirits behind the veil speaking to me. Help me judge a righteous judgement.

DECREE

I decree demonic winds are shuttered out of my mind. I declare the leading of the Holy Spirit brings me into all truth and light and love, in Jesus's name.

March 25

Keep Framing Your World with My Word

I hear you profess, "Greater is He that is in me than he that is in the world." I hear you say these words when you feel victorious. Don't stop professing this truth when you feel like the enemy has painted you in a corner. Keep framing your world with My Word. Keep confessing who you are in Me and who I am in you. Don't let the words of your mouth and the meditations of your heart shift into agreement with the enemy's plans. I am the greater One. Think of me.

HEBREWS 11:3; PSALM 19:14; PROVERBS 12:14

PRAYER

Father, put me in remembrance of Your Word. Help me continually speak forth Your purified Word over the areas of my life where the enemy is working to bring corruption.

DECREE

I decree the enemy's strategies to frame my world are deconstructed. I declare the greater One not only lives inside me, but He empowers me to keep the devil under my feet, in Jesus's name.

Fight with the Prophetic Sword

*T*ake the advice that Paul gave to his spiritual son Timothy. Wage war with the prophecies—the genuine prophecies—spoken over your life. Don't merely receive a prophetic word, put it in a drawer, and hope it comes to pass. Don't ignore the prophetic promptings that I've given you. Record and review My inspiration. Fight with the prophetic sword I've put in your hands. The enemy is warring against your prophecy. War with it and watch it come to pass in My due time.

1 TIMOTHY 1:18; EPHESIANS 6:17; MATTHEW 4:4

PRAYER

Father, thank You for speaking over my life. Help me discipline my spirit to use the prophetic sword as a weapon to annihilate the opposition to Your revealed will in my life.

DECREE

I decree the God-inspired prophecies spoken over my life shall come to pass. I declare the resistance to God's calling and election on my life is cut to pieces, in Jesus's name.

Don't Let Frustration Take You Off Track

Stop allowing the enemy to disrupt your flow. Don't let frustration take you off track. Refuse to let disappointment set you back. When fear comes knocking at your door as you transition, don't answer it. Too many times you are allowing the wicked one access to your life, and the end result is delay or derailment. You have the authority to shut him out of your mind, your mouth, your finances, your relationships, and anything else I've given you to steward. Shut him out!

PHILIPPIANS 4:6–7; LUKE 10:19; LUKE 9:1–2

PRAYER

Father, forgive me for allowing the devil any place in my mind. I rebuke the spirit of fear that has been hanging out in the atmosphere over my life, in Jesus's name.

DECREE

I decree the enemy is forbidden from entering my territory. I declare his access is shut off, shut down, and shut out, and his huffing and puffing won't blow my house down, in Jesus's name.

I Am Your Strong Tower

I am your refuge in times of trouble. My name is a strong tower. Run into Me and find safety. Run into My presence when you feel like you can't take another step. Rest in Me when your enemies seem to have you surrounded. I will not let go of you. I will not let you down. I am for you and against the enemy of your soul. Here's what I am saying: trust me in the warfare the same way you trust Me beside the still waters. I am your God. I am for you.

PROVERBS 18:10; PSALM 61:3; PSALM 91:2

PRAYER

Father, I take refuge in You. Teach me how to rest and hold on to Your promises. Teach me to dwell in Your strong tower perpetually. Help me trust You.

DECREE

I decree the enemy of my life is cut down like stubble. I declare my Lord leads me beside still waters and makes me lie down in green pastures, in Jesus's name.

Don't Make Room for Enemy Interference

Don't think about what you're going say before you get to the confrontation. I'm going to put My words in your mouth. Don't get into vain imaginations about the confrontations but believe Me because I'm going to tell you what to say. Don't you think I know what you should say? Don't you think I know what they are going to say? Stop trying to figure it out because you are making room for enemy interference. Believe Me, and My joy will sustain you even in the midst of the confrontation you're dreading.

LUKE 12:12; EXODUS 4:12; PROVERBS 15:1

PRAYER

Father, I exalt You as the omniscient God. Teach me what to say in every confrontation with people or demon powers. Put Your words in my mouth and I will speak.

DECREE

I decree vain imaginations into the enemy's strategy meeting over my life. I declare I carry the joy of the Lord into every confrontation, in Jesus's name.

Don't Defend Yourself

When people rise up against you with harsh words, remain silent until you hear My voice. When people make accusations against you, don't defend yourself. Let Me defend you. Remember that the enemy will use any ungodly words you say against you in the heat of the moment. Let the situation settle. Wait for My peace to come upon you before responding, and realize that sometimes the best response is no response at all. Pray and allow Me time to convict them instead of escalating the enemy's plans with harsh words of your own.

PSALM 46:10; LAMENTATIONS 3:26; PROVERBS 29:11

PRAYER

Father, set a guard over my mouth so I will not be tempted to speak out of turn. Holy Spirit, tame my tongue so I don't release deadly poison into my life.

DECREE

I decree my tongue is the pen of a ready writer, and I release healing words of the Lord. I declare my mouth shall not transgress in the presence of the Lord, in Jesus's name.

I Can Hold You Together

I hold the entire world together. Don't you think I can hold you together? I know the fire is hot. I know the war against your mind is raging. I see the enemy attacks. Here's your strategy: stick closer to Me. When your friends and enemies rise up against you, I will still be standing by your side. When all forsake you in the battle, I will still be there to lead you through. I hold the entire world together; I can hold you together. Grab hold of Me and don't let go. You win.

JAMES 4:8; HEBREWS 13:5; PSALM 18:48

PRAYER

Father, draw me close to You and never let me go. Don't relax Your hold on me for a moment. Help me hold myself together when the war seems too much for me.

DECREE

I decree every enemy attempt to break me down is burned up in God's all-consuming fire. I declare if my mother and father forsake me, the Lord is with me, in Jesus's name.

APRIL

*Do not be afraid, you beasts of the field; for the
open pastures are springing up, and the tree bears
its fruit; the fig tree and the vine yield their
strength. Be glad then, you children of Zion, and
rejoice in the Lord your God; for He has given you
the former rain faithfully, and He will cause the
rain to come down for you—the former rain, and
the latter rain in the first month. The threshing
floors shall be full of wheat, and the vats shall
overflow with new wine and oil.*

JOEL 2:22–24

April 1

Be Slower to Speak

Be slow to speak. Be slower to speak. Many times I watch you open your mouth wide to express what you do not like. Don't complain about what you don't like. Complaining is like a snare of the enemy. He snares you with the words of your mouth. If you can't praise Me, if you can't thank Me, if you can't release words of life, then keep your mouth tightly shut up until you can. Ask Me to set a guard over your mouth. I will help you overcome the temptation to complain if you ask Me.

JAMES 1:19; PHILIPPIANS 2:14; PSALM 141:3

PRAYER

Father, cause me to bite my tongue when I start to speak out of turn. Give me a red light in my spirit when I need to keep my mouth shut or stop speaking, and I will obey You.

DECREE

I decree no corrupt communication in agreement with the enemy of my soul shall escape my lips. I declare my words bring life and light to those who hear them, in Jesus's name.

April 2

Avoid the Spirit of Competition

*W*hy are there wars and envies among you? If you need something, won't I provide it? If you want something, why not just ask Me? Avoid the spirit of competition because it is a gateway to the spirit of strife. Where strife rises up, you have created an atmosphere where confusion and every evil work will dominate. Strife kills the anointing. Stop striving for what you think you want and ask Me to give you what you need. When others want to play tug-of-war with you, let go of the rope and walk in peace.

PHILIPPIANS 2:3–4; JAMES 3:14–16; GALATIANS 5:19–23

PRAYER

Father, help me avoid strife like I would avoid the plague, because that's what it is. Show me clearly the danger of this enemy so I won't go near it or agree with it.

DECREE

I decree the spirit of competition is cut off from my midst. I declare strife has no place in me, and it will not work through me or against me, in Jesus's name.

Don't Act Like Your Enemy

Don't swap railing for railing. Don't repay evil with evil. The enemy works through people. You can't see him. You only see the people he's using as weapons against you. Your best defense is an offense—submit yourself to Me and resist him. When you return evil for evil, you are not submitting to Me, for My Word instructs a better way. Turn the other cheek. Walk the extra mile. Move in the opposite spirit. Then you are walking in Christ.

1 PETER 3:9; JAMES 4:7; MATTHEW 5:38–40

PRAYER

Father, help me resist the temptation to react to the people who the enemy is using. Help me to remember to rise up and take authority over the spirits and love the people.

DECREE

I decree evil has no power over me. I declare I will walk in love for people; I will push back the enemy and walk in Christ, in Jesus's name.

Don't Let the Enemy Cast You Out

*N*ever allow the enemy to cast you out of your calling. Too many of My children are aborting their calling in the face of enemy attack. You have an anointing to cast out devils. You have an anointing to plow through enemy opposition. You have an anointing to break the yokes that the wicked one has secured around your neck. Don't allow the enemy to cast you down. Rise up and cast him out, then slam the door shut and lock it. Refuse to allow him entrance into your mind, will, and emotions. Continually cast down thoughts that are not pure and lovely and of a good report, and you'll cast out the enemy.

MARK 16:17; 2 CORINTHIANS 10:5; ISAIAH 10:27

PRAYER

Father, give me the courage to keep on pressing into my high calling. Help me walk worthy of my calling instead of walking away when the heat is on.

DECREE

I decree the enemy's attempts to bring forced abortion to my call are canceled. I declare I carry a yoke-breaking, burden-removing anointing that sets captives free, in Jesus's name.

April 5

Don't Walk on the Edge

*F*rustration is an open door to fear. When you allow yourself to get frustrated, you open the gate wide to demonic imaginations. You fear you will not overcome. You doubt anything will ever change. You walk on the edge of explosive anger. Choose faith instead. You can't walk in frustration and walk in faith at the same time. You'll need faith to combat the enemy assignment that is frustrating you. Do not fear and do not fret. Walk in faith. I am still in control.

JOHN 16:33; 1 PETER 5:7; PSALM 37:1

PRAYER

Father, help me stem the tide of frustration that races in my mind and rages against my soul when the enemy starts meddling. Help me hand You the reins and walk in peace.

DECREE

I decree demonic imaginations are captured and cast out of my mind. I declare my mind is full of peace, joy, and love, and frustration has no room, in Jesus's name.

April 6

See Me As the Greater One

See me as larger than your enemies, as larger than life—because I am. I am the Almighty God. I am bigger than, stronger than, and greater than every spiritual foe. No demon power can stand against me. Stop looking at yourself like a grasshopper—like you are smaller than, weaker than, and lesser than. You are in Me and I am in you. When you lean on me and not on your own understanding, you will find the strategies you need to succeed in every battle.

1 JOHN 4:4; NUMBERS 13:33; PROVERBS 3:5–6

PRAYER

Father, help me overcome the grasshopper mentality in every area of my life and see myself in You. Help me understand that when I am weak, You are strong.

DECREE

I decree my spiritual foes slip down the slope of their own pride. I declare I live and move and have my being in the greater One, in Jesus's name.

April 7

Watch Your Mouth

Let no corrupt communication come out of your mouth for in doing so you are opening a gate for the enemy to walk through to kill, steal, and destroy. I've warned you about the power of death and life in your tongue. Heed my warning because your adversary the devil comes for your words. He comes looking for your agreement to wreak havoc on your life. He will use your words as weapons against you if you let him. So watch your mouth and speak only that which is edifying.

EPHESIANS 4:29; PROVERBS 18:21; 1 PETER 3:10

PRAYER

Father, set a guard over my mouth and let my tongue cleave to the roof of my mouth if I set out to speak anything against Your will. Help me tame my tongue.

DECREE

I decree the power of life issues a death warrant against the enemy's plans. I declare the power of life emanates from my tongue and brings healing, in Jesus's name.

April 8

Rule Your Own Spirit

*Y*ou are a spirit, but you must maintain rule over your spirit. Take care what you allow in your eye gates and ear gates that will defile you. Walk in love and peace and avoid anger and wrath. Put all malice away from you. For he who has no rule over his spirit is like a city that is broken down and without walls. Rebuild the walls around you by repenting—changing the way you think and walking with My Spirit rather than in the flesh.

PSALM 101:3; PROVERBS 25:28; GALATIANS 5:16

PRAYER

Father, give me a greater revelation that I am a spirit who has a soul and lives in a body. Give me strength in my inner man to walk in love and peace and rule my spirit.

DECREE

I decree my spirit man follows the leadership of the Holy Spirit who lives on the inside of me. I declare that my spirit is strong in Christ and resists enemy attack, in Jesus's name.

When You Face a Lack Attack

When you are facing a lack attack, you have to hit back with a seed. Let your seed become a weapon and your sowing an act of war. The enemy doesn't want you to cast your bread on many waters. He wants you to devour your future by eating your seed. Know this: when the enemy attacks you in the realm of your finances, you can sow your way out. You can choose to let your seed express your faith in My ability to provide all your needs according to My riches in glory. You can let your seed battle for you in the spirit by faith. Sow!

2 Corinthians 9:6; Ecclesiastes 11:6; Genesis 26:12

PRAYER

Father, help me avoid the temptation to eat my seed when the voice of lack is screaming in my ear. Show me when and where to sow, and I will obey You.

DECREE

I decree double fire consumes every lack attack against my life. I declare everything I put my hand to prospers and I walk in supernatural prosperity, in Jesus's name.

It's Never Too Late

It's never too late because I'm never late. So when you feel like the world is crashing all around you, know it won't be long before I come crashing in on the situation that's burdening you. I will not let more come upon you than you can bear. I always provide a way of escape. You will see My way of escape more clearly when you unburden yourself. Your spiritual vision will improve when you stop looking at what the enemy is doing and look at what I have already done in your life in past seasons. I will show up for you again. Believe Me.

ECCLESIASTES 3:11; 2 CORINTHIANS 10:3; ISAIAH 43:18–19

PRAYER

Father, help me see Jesus clearly in the midst of the warfare. Help me focus on Jesus as the way of escape and wait for the words of the Holy Spirit to show me the strategy.

DECREE

I decree the enemy's blinding tactics cannot affect my spiritual eyes. I declare my God is never late to the battle and always leads me into triumph in Christ, in Jesus's name.

Step Into My Times and Seasons

$\mathcal{N}$ot all days are created equal. Not all times and seasons are the same. There's a time for peace and a time for war. You have to step into My times and seasons to see your prophetic destiny fulfilled, but that enemy of yours—and of Mine—wants to disrupt your times and seasons. He uses fear to keep you from stepping out. He uses unbelief to keep you from following through. Don't make peace with your fear and unbelief. Wage war against it. You can cast it down and walk in My will.

ECCLESIASTES 3:1; PSALM 31:14–15

PRAYER

Father, help me discern the times and seasons of my life so I can move in lockstep with Your Spirit. Help me detect the voice of unbelief that keeps me from moving in faith.

DECREE

I decree enemies of my promotion are demoted to a place under my feet as I ascend. I declare I move according to God's timing and on His calendar for His glory, in Jesus's name.

I See the Enemy Plots Against You

I see the end from the beginning, so don't you think I saw the enemy plotting this attack against you? I am not shocked, dismayed, or overwhelmed by this. The plots, plans, and schemes of the enemy do not move Me. I know you are shocked, dismayed, and overwhelmed in the heat of the battle, but don't let that move you off My Word. My Word is an anchor for your soul. It anchors your emotions and will settle your heart. You may not have seen it coming, but I did. I am a warrior, and I will help you fight your battles.

ISAIAH 46:10; PROVERBS 15:3; HEBREWS 6:19

PRAYER

Father, You see all things and know all things. Would You show me things to come? Would You help me see clear through the enemy's smoke and mirrors of deception?

DECREE

I decree the plots, plans, and schemes of the enemy are foiled by the spirit of grace at work in my life. I declare my soul is anchored by the Word of God, in Jesus's name.

April 13

I Have Your Back

You've heard it said that you should not run from your enemy because the armor I've given you for battle only protects you while you are aggressively on the offensive stance. It's true that your armor covers your front end and that you should not run from the battle line. But know that I am your rear guard. As you move forward in My grace to battle, I have your back. I have you covered. So advance now and do not fear. I am your 360-degree shield.

ISAIAH 52:12; ISAIAH 58:8; DEUTERONOMY 33:29

PRAYER

Father, give me supernatural courage like David had to run to the battle line and take on Goliath. Help me trust that You will surround me with angels, favor, and grace in the war.

DECREE

I decree the enemy's attempts to sneak up on me from behind are obstructed by the Spirit of God. I declare God is my rear guard and goes before me, in Jesus's name.

April 14

When the Enemy Bombards Your Mind

I've given you the helmet of salvation. Put it on. Strap it on tightly. For your enemy wants you to question the hope of your salvation. The enemy wants to bombard you with thoughts that aim to rattle you. The enemy wants you to forget who you are in Christ. The helmet of salvation with which I have equipped you will help you guard your heart and mind in Christ Jesus. Remember the joy of your salvation and the benefits of our covenant and resist the lies of the wicked one.

EPHESIANS 6:17; COLOSSIANS 1:27; PSALM 51:12

PRAYER

Father, thank You for the helmet of salvation. Help me resist the temptation to take it off and lay it down and open myself up to attacks on my identity in Christ.

DECREE

I decree the lies about my identity rebound off my helmet of salvation. I declare my helmet of salvation is secure and I walk in revelation of who I am in Christ, in Jesus's name.

April 15

Walk in a Different Spirit

*C*aleb and Joshua had a different spirit. When the Israelite spies went to see the Promised Land, they saw the giant grapes, but they also saw the giants and they allowed fear to enter their heart. Caleb and Joshua had a different spirit. They had a spirit of faith, and My spirit of might enabled them to enter the Promised Land and rout their enemies little by little. Embrace the spirit of faith, fight the good fight and little by little, you will see your enemies flee.

NUMBERS 14:24; 2 CORINTHIANS 4:13; ISAIAH 11:12

PRAYER

Father, give me a spirit like Joshua and Caleb—a spirit that is unintimidated, a spirit that is fearless in the face of enemy taunt, a spirit of faith.

DECREE

I decree every giant in my promised land is bound and evicted now. I declare by faith that I am walking into the promises God gave me in His Word, in Jesus's name.

April 16

Let It Rain

The enemy will throw stones at you and kick up dust in your face. Don't allow that to distract you. Stay the course. Keep on walking in your assignment. Don't react or respond to the stone throwing and dust flinging. Don't answer your accusers with accusations or throw dust back into their camp. The dust will settle. The more you engage with the whirlwind, the longer it will take to settle. Look to Me. Call for the rain. The rain always causes the dust to settle. This is your prayer, "Let it rain."

2 SAMUEL 16:13; JOEL 2:23; MATTHEW 27:12

PRAYER

Father, sometimes it's hard to see when the enemy is kicking up dust of accusations, imaginations, and lies. Help me see through the subterfuge and walk in Your ways.

DECREE

I decree every stone the enemy throws at me will be returned to him with supernatural force. I declare the rain of God washes away the residue of warfare, in Jesus's name.

April 17

Prophesy to the Dry Bones

Prophesy to the dry bones in your life. Prophesy the resurrection of the dead things, those things the enemy killed. Prophesy the rekindling of the fire that once burned brighter inside of you before the onslaught of spiritual warfare. Prophesy that your latter shall be greater than your past. Prophesy to the wind. Prophesy to yourself. Prophesy out loud so your faith in what I say about you rises with every word you utter. Prophesy.

EZEKIEL 7:1–14; JOB 8:7; PSALM 116:10

PRAYER

Father, give me the words to speak to the dry bones in my life so I can prophesy rightly. Help me not to get discouraged in the face of those situations that seem dead.

DECREE

I decree every dry bone in my life is rustling and resurrecting by the power of the Holy Spirit. I declare my prophetic utterances bring life to dire circumstances, in Jesus's name.

April 18

Love Become a Weapon

*W*hen the enemy targets your relationships for attack, love becomes a sharp weapon. Walking in love gives you the upper hand against the enemy that's working to devour your divine connections. Christ walked the earth as the Word made flesh. Christ is love. Walk in the Word, and you are walking in love. Don't fall for the temptation to answer rashly or defend yourself. When you walk in love, you will always find Me on your side.

EPHESIANS 5:2; PSALM 119:105; GALATIANS 5:25

PRAYER

Father, help me walk in love. Inspire me by Your great love for me to return love to even the ones who are acting hateful toward me. Help me act like Jesus.

DECREE

I decree the Word frames every aspect of my life and makes no room for the enemy. I declare I am crucified with Christ and it is no longer I who live but Christ who lives in me, in Jesus's name.

April 19

I Am the God of Justice

I know you hate injustice. I hate injustice. I am a God of justice. I can make the wrong things right and the crooked places straight. Stop spending so much time seeking your own justice. Instead spend that fervent energy on helping those who are less fortunate than you obtain justice. Set your mind on making this world a better place for those who are less fortunate. Take on social justice works. I will work things out for you in the meantime.

PROVERBS 21:15; AMOS 5:24; ZECHARIAH 7:9

PRAYER

Father, give me justice against my enemies. Lord, avenge me against my spiritual foes who have worked to kill, steal, and destroy my life. Vindicate me for Your glory.

DECREE

I decree every injustice is reversed in my life into overwhelming displaces of mercy. I declare injustices are turned into justice against the enemy of my soul, in Jesus's name.

April 20

The Fight to Prosper

Poverty is not just a mind-set. It's a spirit that seeks to kill your prosperity—your ability to be a blessing to others. When the voice of poverty speaks to your heart and shouts at your mind, lean into Me. I have promised to supply all your needs. I am not a poor God. I own everything, and if I don't have something you need, I can create it for you. Stop allowing the spirit of poverty to rob your inheritance. Rise up, fight and prosper.

PHILIPPIANS 4:19; MATTHEW 6:31–32; LUKE 12:24

PRAYER

Father, let Your Word renew my mind rapidly in the area of finances so the enemy of my wealth can no longer intimidate me with threats against my welfare.

DECREE

I decree the voice of poverty is silenced in my atmosphere. I declare the spirit called poverty is overwhelmed by God's plans to bring divine prosperity, in Jesus's name.

See Yourself Through the Lens of Heaven

Come up higher. See Me as I am. See yourself as you are. See the things around and about you as they truly are, not as the enemy paints them. See the blessings. See the warfare. See it all—everything I'm trying to show you. See it. See it. See it. See it. See it. See it. See it. See it through My eyes, through the lens of Heaven. See it from My perspective. Don't allow the enemy to skew your vision.

COLOSSIANS 3:2; 2 CORINTHIANS 4:18; 2 PETER 3:8–9

PRAYER

Father, let me see myself through Your eyes, the eyes of love, instead of the enemy's accusations and condemnations. Show me who I really am in Christ.

DECREE

I decree the enemy's vision into my life is skewed. I declare I am seated in heavenly places, far above all principalities and powers that work to pervert my vision of myself, in Jesus's name.

April 22

Push Back the Darkness That Tries to Blind You

I've given you weapons to battle the wicked one with. I've given you spiritual arsenal to push back the darkness that tries to blind you from the light of My truth. I've given you firepower. But the weapons I've given you are spiritual weapons, not carnal weapons. Always remember, you fight by faith and not by the flesh. Fight the good fight of faith with your spiritual weapons and resist the temptation to fight in your flesh. In your flesh, you are no match for the enemy of your soul. But when you fight in My Spirit with My weapons, you are unconquerable. So get out of your flesh and into faith, and you will see swift victory over your foes.

2 Corinthians 10:4; Psalm 7:13; Jeremiah 10:5

PRAYER

Father, help me to keep my flesh under the power of Your spirit so it doesn't cloud my mind and weaken my will. Teach me to walk in faith and not in flesh.

DECREE

I decree my spiritual weapons overpower the weapons the enemy is using to provoke my flesh. I declare I walk by faith and not by sight, flesh, or imaginations.

Be Quick to Recognize You're Wounded

The enemy will work to inflict a wound on the strongest of souls to make it the weakest. Emotional wounds weaken the soul and break down defenses. Be quick to recognize a soul wound. Be quick to run to the Father and seek healing. The enemy's strategy is to tempt you to agree with his lies in an especially vulnerable time. Do not be ignorant of this device. Guard your heart from hurts and wounds. Decide to believe the best, and when you can't, run to love. Love casts out wounds if you let it. Cast your wound on Father and let His love heal your wounded soul, then rise up and fight again.

PSALM 147:3; JEREMIAH 17:14; PSALM 6:6–9

PRAYER

Father, pour out Your healing balm of Gilead over my soul and restore any areas of my heart that are wounded. Let Your love confront my hurt and pain.

DECREE

I decree every enemy device and agenda to tempt me into sin in the midst of my pain is broken. I declare emotional healing is my portion, in Jesus's name.

April 24

Surrender Your All to Me

Stop giving your will to the enemy. Stop surrendering to his thoughts. Stop surrendering to his will. Stop surrendering to his plans and his agenda and his whispers that come against your mind, but surrender your mind to Me. Surrender your soul completely to Me. Surrender your will, surrender your emotions, surrender your imagination, surrender your reasoning, surrender your intellect, surrender all that you have and everything you are and all that you do to Me, and you will walk in a measure of victory that you have not yet fully seen.

LUKE 9:23–24; GALATIANS 2:20; ROMANS 12:1

PRAYER

Father, forgive me for surrendering any part of me to the enemy's will. Restore my soul. Strengthen my resolve. Set a flame upon my heart. I am Yours.

DECREE

I decree every stronghold of the enemy in my mind is broken. I declare my heart, my mind, my will, my emotions, and my imaginations are submitted to God, in Jesus's name.

April 25

Don't Fear the Enemy

The enemy can smell fear, just like a dog. Don't fear the enemy. He has no authority over you. Rather, you have authority over him. Take Paul's advice to the church at Philippi—don't be frightened in any way, shape, or form by those who oppose you. Don't be afraid of people and their words. Don't be afraid of the enemy and his threats. Don't be intimidated by your spiritual foes. This is a sign to them that they will be destroyed, but I will save you!

PHILIPPIANS 1:28; COLOSSIANS 1:16–17; 2 TIMOTHY 1:7

PRAYER

Father, help me not to cower in the face of enemy threats. Help me rise up with the boldness of a lion against the roaming lion that's seeking to devour me.

DECREE

I decree the enemy's intimidation tactics are impotent against me. I declare that I will not bow to fear, but I will stand against it and overcome it, in Jesus's name.

When the Enemy Steals Your Time

When the enemy puts you in a demonic time warp—stealing hours and even days of your life—remember this: I can help you make up for lost time. I will open a divine time warp and redeem the time for you if you trust Me. Don't get anxious about the looming deadlines and don't get overwhelmed by the enemy's pressure. Stop worrying about what is not getting done and trust that My grace is sufficient. I can redeem the time for you as you stay steadily focused on My goodness. I am the author of time, and your times are in My hands. Ask Me to redeem your time.

PSALM 31:15; PROVERBS 12:25; JOHN 14:27

PRAYER

Father, You hold my times in Your hands, and the enemy is working overtime to rob what precious little I have. Help me discern the time-stealing devices of the enemy.

DECREE

I decree every demonic time warp in operation in my life is shattered. I declare my God redeems my time supernaturally for His glory, in Jesus's name.

April 27

Armor Up!

Sometimes the reason the enemy is hitting you is because you forgot to put your armor on. You neglected to get dressed for war in the morning, to put on Christ, to put on the robe of righteousness, to put on the cloak of zeal. But it's not too late. It's never too late to embrace My whole armor. So, take a moment and consider each element of My armor and get dressed for the battle. The enemy cannot penetrate My armor. He will try but he will fail. Remember who you are and the authority you carry, then armor up and run to the battle line expecting a sweeping victory.

EPHESIANS 6:10–18; ISAIAH 59:17; ROMANS 13:12–14

PRAYER

Father, help me not to take the war lightly but to get dressed for battle each and every day. Give me a greater revelation of the armor You have given me.

DECREE

I decree the cloak of zeal and the robe of righteousness confounds the stratagem of the wicked one. I declare I am protected by God's very own armor, in Jesus's name.

I Am Your Light in Dark Places

I am your rock, your fortress, your deliverer. Run to Me and take refuge in Me when the enemy is hurling darts and spewing lies to bind you up. I am your shield and your salvation. I am your light in the dark places. Call upon My name and I will hear you and rescue you from the pit of lies the enemy has trapped you in. You will see and know the truth, and the truth will set you free as you choose to listen to My voice in the secret place. Run to Me.

PSALM 18:2; PSALM 62:6; JEREMIAH 29:12

PRAYER

Father, I am calling on Your holy name even now. Help me see the truth that sets me free from the lies and darkness that are invading my soul.

DECREE

I decree the adder spewing lies at me chokes on his own poison. I declare God is my light, my rock, my fortress, my deliverer, and my salvation, in Jesus's name.

April 29

I Will Put Words in Your Mouth

I am the One who guarantees you the victory. I am the One who will put the words in your mouth for that confrontation that you're dreading. I am the One who will give you the strength to walk through the day, not just barely getting by, but overcoming every obstacle that the enemy puts in your path. I am the One who gives you wisdom for life, wisdom for wealth, wisdom for relationships. Wisdom, wisdom, wisdom. Ask of Me, and I will pour it out to you liberally. I am not going to leave you without help. I am your helper, and I am very present anytime you call upon Me.

EXODUS 15:2; JAMES 1:5; PROVERBS 2:6

PRAYER

Father, put Your words in my mouth, and I will execute judgment on every spiritual foe. Give me wisdom for the warfare so I can see through the dread.

DECREE

I decree the vibration of my voices causes the enemy of my soul to shake and rattle in fear. I declare God is with me and for me in every battle, in Jesus's name.

April 30

Don't Buy Into the Lying Vanities

*D*on't buy into lying vanities—symptoms of aches, pains, and disease that afflict your body. The enemy is a master of lies and deception. He wants to destroy your health. He wants to fool you into accepting aches, pains, sicknesses, and diseases. Don't buy into the lie. Resist the symptoms. Pray and break enemy afflictions. Meditate on My healing Word. Confess that you are healed. Don't answer the door and receive the enemy's package. Slam the door shut!

JONAH 2:8; 1 PETER 2:24; 3 JOHN 2

PRAYER

Father, help me be quick to recognize and reject the enemy's lying vanities and subtle suggestions to my soul. Help me fight off sickness like it's a devil, because it is.

DECREE

I decree the wicked devices of infirmity return to his own head. I declare the enemy's destructive desires for my life shall not land, in Jesus's name.

MAY

For though we walk in the flesh, we do not war according to the flesh. For the weapons of our warfare are not carnal but mighty in God for pulling down strongholds, casting down arguments and every high thing that exalts itself against the knowledge of God, bringing every thought into captivity to the obedience of Christ, and being ready to punish all disobedience when your obedience is fulfilled.

2 CORINTHIANS 10:3–6

May 1

Mark the Dividers Among You

Mark those among you who cause division. Beware of those who sow seeds of discord. These acts of spiritual violence breed witchcraft and pain. Choose to walk in such a level of peace and in such an alert spirit that you quickly discern dividers, detractors, and distractors who pull you out of My presence and My will. Pluck up the seeds of discord that have been sown in your soul. Slam the door on gossip and slander. Repent of agreeing with the accuser of the brethren and bless those who have cursed you.

ROMANS 16:17; 1 CORINTHIANS 1:10–13; TITUS 3:9–11

PRAYER

Father, help me see clearly those who sow discord in my midst so I can beware coming into any form of agreement. Mute me if I am tempted to gossip.

DECREE

I decree every spirit of division working against me falls to the shield of unity I have erected around me. I declare the words of my mouth sow peace, in Jesus's name.

Slam the Door on Offense

Slam the door on offense. Stop giving ear to the spirit that wants to destroy your life. For offense is a deadly tool in the enemy's box. He pulls it out at opportune times to cause you to shut the door on relationships, leave churches, and otherwise disconnect from people and places I've called you to be. Remember this, you can't walk in offense without walking in unforgiveness. Don't take the bait and end up in bondage. Choose to believe the best and pray for those who have wronged you.

PROVERBS 19:11; MATTHEW 18:15–17; LUKE 17:3–4

PRAYER

Father, help me cultivate a spirit that is sensitive to Yours so that when any other spirit tries to speak to my heart, to deceive my soul, I will not follow it.

DECREE

I decree the subtle voice of offense is muted in my life. I declare I am unoffendable and unforgiveness has no place in my heart, in Jesus's name.

Quench the Enemy's Fire with My Word

When the enemy sets your field on fire, quench the raging inferno with My Word. There are three that agree: the water, the Spirit, and the blood. Let the water of My Word lick up the flames of the evil one. Speak My Word into the situation and watch the enemy's plans drown in the overflow of your faith-filled, Sprit-led decrees. Plead the blood of Jesus over everything that belongs to you. Take a stand for your field and command the enemy to leave, in Christ's name.

ISAIAH 55:11; PROVERBS 30:5; ISAIAH 40:8

PRAYER

Father, strengthen my arms so I can keep my shield of faith lifted high and quench all the fiery darts of the enemy. Give me new boldness to speak Your Word with authority.

DECREE

I decree the release of double fire against the enemy of my soul. I declare the blood of Jesus cleanses and protects me from unrighteousness, in Jesus's name.

Get Thee Behind Me, Satan!

Tell the enemy of your soul: Get behind me! Many times you give the enemy a place in your life he doesn't deserve. You give him attention he craves, like a spoiled child who demands to be heard. You give him the glory that belongs to Me by your constant gaze upon his work. Don't be ignorant of the enemy's plots and plans. But don't put him in the center of your focus. Like Jesus, issue the command, "Get behind me!" and keep going. I have your back.

MATTHEW 16:23; 2 CORINTHIANS 2:11; PHILIPPIANS 1:28

PRAYER

Father, help me discern the enemy sneaking into my presence like a slithering snake with a voice and lies like poisonous venom. Help me watch and pray.

DECREE

I decree the enemy is under my feet because Christ is the head of all principalities and powers. I declare I'm the head and not the tail, above and not beneath, in Jesus's name.

Beware Operating in a Rash Spirit

Don't walk in a rash spirit. Rash words cut and hurt people, including yourself. Rash decisions can put you on the wrong side of My will for your life. The safest place for you is in the center of my will. Rash and harsh words grieve My Spirit and lead you out of My will instead of deeper into it. Hold your peace when you feel like responding rashly. Wait on Me for wisdom when you feel like making rash decisions. You'll avoid much spiritual warfare this way.

ECCLESIASTES 5:2; ACTS 19:36; PROVERBS 12:18

PRAYER

Father, restrain my lips from opening to release rash words out of my mouth. I don't want to grieve Your spirit. Warn me when I am about to make rash decisions.

DECREE

I decree my mouth utters words of the wise that push back darkness from my life. I declare I wait on the Lord before speaking, acting, or moving, in Jesus's name.

Ask Me for the Grace of Humility

Humble yourself under My mighty hand. Ask Me for the grace of humility. Refuse to defend yourself against the false accusations apart from My leading. I've instructed you in My Word to submit yourself to Me and resist the devil so he will flee. When you walk in humility, you will find yourself in a position where I can exalt you high above every wagging tongue. I Myself will defend you. I Myself will empower you. Humble yourself. Jesus did.

1 PETER 5:6; JAMES 4:6; PHILIPPIANS 2:8

PRAYER

Father, give me the grace of humility so I can cooperate with Your commands. Help me to resist the temptation to think more highly of myself than I ought.

DECREE

I decree wagging tongues that mutter are cut off from my midst. I declare God will exalt me above my enemies as I bow to His will, in Jesus's name.

The Enemy Has No New Strategies

*Y*ou will always face new levels of warfare. But make no mistake—the enemy has no new strategies. He has no new tactics. He has no new ideas. He has no new weapons. He has no new wisdom. When you face warfare you've never experienced before, listen for My voice. Let Me remind you of these very words. Let this truth saturate your soul. The truth about who you are in Christ and the authority you carry in His name makes you ready and able to stand and withstand at every level of warfare. Mark My words.

1 CORINTHIANS 16:9; JOHN 10:5; EPHESIANS 6:13

PRAYER

Father, give me a hearing ear that I would hear with crystal clarity Your still, small voice even when the enemy is shouting lies to my soul.

DECREE

I decree the enemy's old tricks find no success in my life because I am hiding in God's shadow. I declare the delegated authority I carry brings the enemy's plans to naught, in Jesus's name.

I Am Not Condemning You

I am not your condemner. I am your justifier. Who is it who condemns? It is Jesus, the Christ, the Son of the living God. But Christ is not condemning you. He justified you. He redeemed you from the curse of the law. He laid His own sinless life down for you. So don't allow condemnation to shape your view of Me or your view of yourself. There is therefore now no condemnation to those who are in Christ Jesus, and you are in Christ Jesus. See yourself in Christ as I do. Separate your actions from your being. Silence the voice of condemnation with a declaration of My love.

JOHN 3:17; 1 JOHN 3:20; ROMANS 8:34

PRAYER

Father, flood my heart with Your pure love so I can distinguish between the Holy Spirit's sting of conviction and the enemy's arrows of condemnation.

DECREE

I decree condemnation into the enemy's camp of spiritual convicts. I declare condemnation is not my portion and the blood of Jesus speaks a better thing over my life, in Jesus's name.

May 9

Receive Grace to Endure the Battle

*M*ake no mistake. Grace will not prevent spiritual warfare against you. Grace will help you endure the warfare until you see the fullness of the victory Christ died to give you. Grace will empower you to execute Christ's will against the enemy. Paul suffered from a thorn in his flesh, a messenger of satan. Three times He asked the Father to remove it from him. The thorn remained. Father told him words you need to remember: My grace is sufficient for you. Where you are weak, I am strong. Stand in grace.

EPHESIANS 2:8–9; JOHN 1:16; 2 TIMOTHY 4:22

PRAYER

Father, give me a balanced perspective of grace in an age when people are perverting Your Word. Help me embrace Your grace to run the race.

DECREE

I decree the unlimited grace of God empowers me to fight the good fight of faith without fail. I declare grace and mercy follow me all the days of my life, in Jesus's name.

May 10

When You Face Slander
for Christ's Sake

*A*postles and prophets in My Word faced slander as they set out on their missions. Jesus Himself faced slander while He was walking the earth and is still shamelessly slandered today. Don't be surprised when unbelievers—or even believers who don't know Me the way you do—slander you for following My will. Let them speak falsely against you for Christ's sake and forgive them. Bless them. Act like your Father in Heaven, and the enemy will gain no advantage over you.

PSALM 101:5; 1 PETER 3:16; MATTHEW 5:11

PRAYER

Father, help me hold my tongue when slander spews forth at my soul. Help me stay steady, unswayable, immovable despite the accusations against my heart.

DECREE

I decree the slander against me disintegrates in the glory atmosphere around me. I declare I will walk like Jesus walked in the face of every false accusation, in Jesus's name.

Tighten Your Belt of Truth

When the enemy is attacking you, tighten your belt of truth one more notch. The truth will guard your mind from the poisonous thoughts the enemy is trying to plant in your soul. The truth will spring up as a harvest of righteousness that will drown out the voice of the wicked one. So, refuse to allow the enemy to strip you of your belt of truth, but instead fasten it securely. Truth is a weapon that never fails to overcome the enemy's most sophisticated, subtle lies.

John 8:32; Ephesians 6:14; Psalm 145:18

PRAYER

Father, help me avoid the slippery slope of deception. Help me keep Your belt of truth tightly fastened around my waist so I do not stray from Your heart.

DECREE

I decree every lie from the pit of hell that has been launched against my mind is abolished. I declare I speak the truth and walk in the truth, in Jesus's name.

A Key to Spiritual Warfare Success

The fear of the Lord is the beginning of wisdom for spiritual warfare. The fear of the Lord will constrain you from entering battles I've not called you to fight. The fear of the Lord will cause you to seek Father's face instead of using the wrong strategy in battle. The fear of the Lord helps you avoid the snares of your adversary. The fear of the Lord opens a place of refuge. The fear of the Lord will cause angels to encamp around you. Don't fear the enemy. Cultivate a reverential fear of the Lord in your heart.

PROVERBS 1:7; MATTHEW 10:28; ECCLESIASTES 12:13

PRAYER

Father, cause me to tremble at Your Word. Teach me to reverence Your Holy Scriptures, which are purified by fire seven times, so I will walk in Your perfect will.

DECREE

I decree ceaseless, supernatural wisdom of God guards and guides my heart in every battle. I declare the fear of man and the fear of the enemy has no place in my heart, in Jesus's name.

May 13

Waging War in the Unseen Realm with Words

*W*hen you call those things that are not as if they exist, you are waging war in the unseen realm and the opposition to My promises in your life. Never underestimate the power of your words. Your heavenly Father called things into existence through His words, which are spirit and life. Abraham called things into existence through his words, which agreed with God. Find out what Father wants to create in your life and use your words to break through the opposition that will surely arise. Speak life.

ROMANS 4:17; PROVERBS 13:3; MATTHEW 12:37

PRAYER

Father, help me talk like You talk. Spur me to keep Your words in my mouth no matter what anything looks like with my natural eyes.

DECREE

I decree victory in the war of words. I declare that my tongue shall not transgress and my mouth releases shouts of deliverance, in Jesus's name.

I Am Dispatching Angels

$\mathcal{I}$m sending angelic assistance your way. I'm dispatching to you angels on assignment just for you. I'm releasing the angels of breakthrough into your life. Don't stop praying now. The angels are coming on assignment because of your words. Don't shrink back from the battle. Help from the heavenly host is on the way. Don't pull back and don't cease fire. You are on the brink of victory. Don't let your foot off the gas. You are speeding forth into triumph. Keep pressing. Keep praying. Angels are encamped around you even now because you fear Me.

PSALM 91; PSALM 103:20; JOSHUA 5:13–14

PRAYER

Father, release Your heavenly host to help me fight against the demon powers that have eyes set on my destruction. Dispatch the warring angels on my behalf.

DECREE

I decree God's angels on assignment overpower every attack against me. I declare angels hearken to the voice of God's Word in my mouth, in Jesus's name.

May 15

I Am Able to Make You Stand in the Shaking

Don't worry because I've strengthened you. You'll make it through just like Peter made it through. When the enemy is shaking you and sifting you, he's trying to move you off the position I've put you in. Stand firm. Stand strong knowing that whatever can be shaken will be shaken, but you shall not be moved. I won't let you go; I've got you in My hand, and I'm able to make you stand in the evil day. I'm able to make you stand in the midst of the battle. I'm able to make you stand when all hell is breaking loose against you; I am able to make you stand.

1 Corinthians 16:13; 1 Corinthians 15:58; 2 Thessalonians 2:15

PRAYER

Father, please strengthen me when I feel like the shaking is going to tear me apart. Frustrate the counsel of the wicked one against my life.

DECREE

I decree hell's attempts to scorch my faith and clothe me with fear and doubt are disassembled. I declare my feet are like hind's feet, in Jesus's name.

I'm Taking the Bitter Sting Away

When you rise up like Job and pray for those who used you, who abused you, who spoke wrongly to you, you will find the healing balm of Gilead released into your heart. You will know and understand that the only One that matters is Me. So stop looking for approval from people and look for My approval, because you'll find that you already have it. Don't look to man for their nod, because I am nodding to you from Heaven. I have given you the nod; I have given you My approval. I have given you My OK. I have given you everything that you need. I am healing your heart even now as you release those who hurt you. I'm taking that bitter sting away.

MATTHEW 5:44; GALATIANS 1:10; COLOSSIANS 3:23

PRAYER

Father, deliver me from the fear of man and people pleasing. Help me find satisfaction, contentment, and joy in pleasing You with my godly deeds.

DECREE

I decree the bitter sting of the enemy returns upon him tenfold. I declare God's love heals my soul as I walk in the grace of forgiveness, in Jesus's name.

Hold On Despite Enemy Interference

*Y*ou belong to Me. I saved you; I paid a price for you. You will not be moved. Just hold on. What I've called you to hold on to will remain with you despite enemy interference. I have you in My grip. You will come out of this stronger. You will come out of this bolder. You will come out of this with more compassion for other people who are going through similar things. You will have a comfort to give them because of the comfort I am giving you now. The enemy wants to make you bitter. But I am making you better.

1 CORINTHIANS 6:20; 2 CORINTHIANS 1:3–5; HEBREWS 12:15

PRAYER

Father, thank You for the shed blood of Your Son, Jesus Christ. Help me never, ever to take His sacrifice lightly. Comfort me with Your love.

DECREE

I decree the enemy's plots to entrap me with resentment are reversed and I am free. I declare I am growing in boldness and compassion, in Jesus's name.

I Am Not Deaf to Your Mayday Cry

When you cry out to Me, I hear you. I am not deaf to your Mayday cry. I do not close My ears to your distress signals through prayer. I see the enemy's shock and awe campaign against you. I hear all the noise he is making in your mind. I know you feel like your faith is being shipwrecked as the raging winds and waves the enemy has stirred up in your life threaten you day and night. But I am a warrior, and My heavenly host is on alert. Continue crying out to Me. I am fighting with you.

PSALM 66:17–20; 1 PETER 3:12; PROVERBS 15:29

PRAYER

Father, thank You for always hearing my cries. My Warrior and my God, reach down Your right hand from Heaven and deliver me from the enemy's snare.

DECREE

I decree the noisy demons hell has sent to harass me are muzzled. I declare my peace holds steady even when the raging winds of the wicked one blows, in Jesus's name.

Hope Against Hope

*A*braham hoped against hope. He had to, and sometime so do you. Always remember, faith is the substance of things hoped for. Once you start looking through the eyes of doubt and unbelief—once you allow your hope to be deferred—you allow the enemy to weaken your faith. You cannot believe without a foundation of hope. I am a God of hope, and despite the bleak outlook in the natural, I know the plans I have for you. My plans for your future are hopeful. Hope in Me.

JEREMIAH 29:11; ROMANS 15:13; ROMANS 4:18–22

PRAYER

Father, let hope come alive in my heart again. Infuse me with hope again. Help me hope in Your goodness when bad things are happening.

DECREE

I decree my hope deferred in past seasons will make way for a sudden good break in the next season. I declare I am a prisoner of hope and hope confines me on every side, in Jesus's name.

May 20

Don't Overthink Things

*E*ven when you can't see Me, even when you can't hear Me, I've got you! I've got your back. I've got your front. I've surrounded you with My angels. They are encamped around you because you believe in My Son and fear My name. Don't worry and don't wonder. Don't overthink things. Just look to My Word because all the answers are right there. All the answers are in Me. Let My Word comfort you in the midst of the pain and renew your mind in the midst of the battle. I've got you.

ISAIAH 26:3; PROVERBS 28:26; ROMANS 12:2

PRAYER

Father, help me shut down my mind and listen to Your heart with the ears of my spirit. Teach me to cast my cares on You, because You care for me.

DECREE

I decree God's light shines on my life and destroys the lies of darkness. I declare my heart trusts in You, and I am helped, in Jesus's name.

May 21

Die to Self to Overcome the Enemy

*C*rucify your flesh instead of fleshing out when the enemy attacks. Die to yourself. Die to your own rights. Stop being so easily offended. Stop getting so mad in an instant. Stop getting so frustrated in a moment and look at Me. Christ is the selfless One, and He modeled the way in spiritual warfare. So, put your flesh down like Jesus put His flesh down. Go low. Decrease that I might increase, and you will see the increase that you've been praying for. I will increase you as you crucify your flesh and walk in the Spirit.

MATTHEW 16:24; ROMANS 6:6; GALATIANS 5:24

PRAYER

Father, give me the grace to crucify my flesh. My spirit is willing, but my flesh is weak. Strengthen me in my inner man and help me die to my selfish desires.

DECREE

I decree the enemies of my flesh stumble and fall when they seek to overcome me. I declare my spirit is strong in the Lord and the power of His might, in Jesus's name.

May 22

I Am the Minister of Supply

I am the minister of supply. I will supply all of your needs in every realm. I will meet every need if you'll look to Me, trust in Me, believe in Me. The enemy can't stop your provision forever. But your doubt can delay it. I'm watching over you carefully, cautiously, warning you, showing you, teaching you, making you, shaping you into the image of My Son so that you can have greater strength, greater peace, and greater joy. The more you yield to Me, the more you become like Me, and the greater is your joy and the greater works you will do.

PHILIPPIANS 4:19; 2 CORINTHIANS 9:8; MATTHEW 7:11

PRAYER

Father, You are my provider, my supplier, the One who watches over me, the giver of life and peace and love. Help me remember that while I'm wrestling the enemy.

DECREE

I decree my God has and will supply all of my needs according to His glorious riches in Christ. I declare my natural, physical, and spiritual needs are met, in Jesus's name.

Stop Allowing Fear Stop Your Ascension

I am taking you higher to levels that will cause you to be so uncomfortable you'll want to run back. You'll want to step down. You'll want to go low. The only thing that's stopping you at this point is your own fear. So, cast out the fear that comes against your faith to go higher. I have given you authority over every devil, the low-level devil and the principality. I've given you authority, and nothing shall by any means harm you, and nothing shall by any means stop you except that which you allow to overtake you. For there is no enemy in the world that is greater than your will. And there's no enemy in the world that's greater than My ability to walk you through into victory.

LUKE 10:19; 1 JOHN 4:4; LUKE 9:1

PRAYER

Father, You have told me over and over and over again not to fear, but somehow subtle fear keeps creeping into my heart. Help me see it and reject it in all its forms.

DECREE

I decree the spirit of fear is tormented by the name of Jesus uttered through my lips. I declare no fear lives here and I am free from fear, in Jesus's name.

Don't Enter Battlefields I Haven't Called You To

Stop standing in gaps that I've not called you to stand in. Get off the walls I've not called you to stand on. For you're taking on warfare and you're taking on enemy fire that I've not called you to sustain. Although I am with you and I love you, I've not called you to fight every battle. Hear the word of the Lord. Don't allow soulish compassion to move you. Let My compassion move you. Jesus did only what He saw the Father do. He could have done many things. He could have gone, here, there, and everywhere, but He only did what He saw the Father do. Let Me lead you into battle.

JOHN 5:19; 2 CORINTHIANS 2:14; 1 SAMUEL 30:8

PRAYER

Father, I don't want to fight battles You have not called me to fight. Help me avoid stepping into the middle of a fray that will bring unnecessary warfare to my life.

DECREE

I decree God has given my enemies into my hand on the battlefield onto which I am called to run. I declare I walk in discernment in the war, in Jesus's name.

The Enemy Is Under Your Feet

*Y*ou've heard it said, "The enemy is under your feet." You've heard it said, "You shall trample on serpents and scorpions and nothing shall by any means harm you." You've read how Joshua instructed his fighting men to put their feet on the necks of the enemies as a sign of their utter defeat. I know it feels at times like the enemy has you under his thumb and that you can't escape the pressure. But remember My Word. Christ is the head of all principalities and powers. You are part of His body. Every enemy is under your feet.

ROMANS 16:20; JOSHUA 10:24; COLOSSIANS 2:10

PRAYER

Father, help me not to respond to the pressure the enemy puts on my mind. Give me the courage to rise up and strike the mark until the enemy falls at my feet.

DECREE

I decree my foot lies on the neck of every enemy who tried to rise up against me. I declare victory over the enemies that tried to trample upon me, in Jesus's name.

May 26

Using Your Blessing as a Weapon

*W*hy do you think Jesus left instructions for you to bless those who curse you? Why do you think Paul the apostle emphasized this principle when he said, "Bless and curse not?" Why do you think your heavenly Father makes the rain to fall and the sun to shine on believers and unbelievers alike? God is good. Use your blessing as a weapon against the enemy's bait of bitterness. Free yourself from resentment by blessing those who have hurt you. I will bless them with a revelation of My love and convict them of their wrong, and you will keep your heart clean in My sight.

ROMANS 12:4; ROMANS 12:20; MATTHEW 7:12

PRAYER

Father, help me resist the temptation to lash back when people use and abuse me. Remind me of the blessing principle and show me how to truly bless my enemies.

DECREE

I decree every spiritual enemy that inspires wicked acts against me is devoured. I declare my acts of blessing perplex the enemy, in Jesus's name.

Goliath Will Fall

*W*hen you face your Goliath—when you face that giant that threatens to kill, steal, and destroy you, remember David. When that giant of sickness and disease threatens to overtake you, run to the battle line with the sword of My Spirit. When a lack attack is trying to break you, tell the enemy what I have to say about your prosperity. When strife enters your relationships, determine to keep your shoes of peace tightly laced up. Whenever Goliath is threatening to take you down, rise up and take it out. You are able in Christ.

MATTHEW 17:20; HEBREWS 11:1; REVELATION 12:11

PRAYER

Father, give me Your vision in the face of the Goliaths that are facing me down. Help me see the opposition from Your perfect perspective, and I will walk in peace.

DECREE

I decree my faith overcomes the world and every giant in it. I declare no giant can prosper against me but instead must bow a knee to God, in Jesus's name.

Shed the Dread

$\mathcal{S}$hed the dread the devil brings to your mind so it doesn't affect your emotions and bend your will. Shed the dread of the week ahead. Shed the dread of the memories of the past that come back to haunt you at inopportune times. Shed the dread of the confrontation. Shed the dread, and embrace My joy, My peace, and My love instead. You don't have to dread, and you don't have to fear, and you don't have to worry. You don't have to walk into situations angry and expecting the worst because I am with you, and I have given you My best. Shed the dread.

GENESIS 9:2; EXODUS 1:12; LEVITICUS 26:6

PRAYER

Father, help me resist the voice of dread and shed the dread that has oppressed my heart. Help me meditate on Your faithfulness and Your peace.

DECREE

I decree the authority I carry causes hell to shake and tremble. I declare I shall not dread the warfare because I have the victory, in Jesus's name.

May 29

Let Me Change You from the Inside Out

𝓘'm working on your heart. I'm working on your flesh. I'm working on your mind. I'm trying to get you out of where you are—that place of discontentment and feeling like nothing is going to change. I'm trying to get your mind on Me. I'm trying to deliver you out of the place of stress and out of that place of torment in your mind because of the enemy's subtle lies. I'm pouring out My Spirit into your spirit. As I work on you, I'm also working on circumstances that defy you. Yield to Me. Let me form you into the image of Christ. Let Me change you from the inside out and everything will change.

2 CORINTHIANS 3:18; PHILIPPIANS 1:6; COLOSSIANS 3:10

PRAYER

Father, work on me. Change me from glory to glory. Remove things in my soul that hinder my total abandon to You and open the door for the enemy's trickery.

DECREE

I decree the enemy trying to change me from the outside in is cast into outer darkness. I declare the circumstances of my life line up with the perfect will of God, in Jesus's name.

Charge Forth Against Old Enemies

Charge forth because My wind is at your back. The enemies that defied you in the past season will now bow because you've come into a new measure of grace. You've come into a new measure of authority. You've come into all of this through the revelation of My heart and the pressing into My love. So, don't be afraid of those things you were once afraid of. Stop being afraid of the enemies of yesterday. Stop worrying about the enemy attacks of tomorrow. Charge forth today and take back the land that the enemy stole.

ISAIAH 61:7; EXODUS 12:36; 2 CHRONICLES 20:25

PRAYER

Father, thank You for Your grace to war. Help me overcome the fear of the past and the enemies that attacked me in the last season and rise up in Your sufficient grace.

DECREE

I decree old enemies fear and shudder at God's Word. I declare I am charging forth and overcoming the enemies of my past for the glory of God, in Jesus's name.

The Enemy Is Grasping at Straws

$\mathcal{D}$on't give up now. You are so close. The enemy has resisted you, but His plans are failing. His plans are faltering. The enemy is grasping at straws. He's losing His grip as you grip your sword a little tighter, like David's mighty man who held on so tight to his weapon that his hand was stuck to the sword when the last enemy fell. Keep holding on to the sword. Keep swinging it. Keep speaking My Word. The enemy will swat at you, but if he comes closer, he will run into the sword and fall at the sword. Don't give up now.

2 Samuel 23:10; Hebrews 4:12; 1 Timothy 6:12

PRAYER

Father, give me the resolve to keep pressing past the enemy's resistance. Help me discern the signs that the enemy is growing weary and the breakthrough is at hand.

DECREE

I decree the enemy cannot maintain his hold on me because the anointing oil causes his thieving hands to slip. I declare "give up" is not in my vocabulary, in Jesus's name.

JUNE

"Behold, I have created the blacksmith who blows the coals in the fire, who brings forth an instrument for his work; and I have created the spoiler to destroy. No weapon formed against you shall prosper, and every tongue which rises against you in judgment you shall condemn. This is the heritage of the servants of the Lord, and their righteousness is from Me," says the Lord.

ISAIAH 54:16–17

June 1

Wear the Cloak of Zeal

Christ wore a cloak of zeal. He is a zealous warrior who never loses a battle. When you are weary, you can choose to put on that same cloak. You can operate in fervent faith. You can choose to rise up with a passion and urgency to dismantle the devil's work against your life. But you have to put on the cloak. You have to stir yourself up. You have to build yourself up in your most holy faith, praying in the spirit and encouraging yourself in My Word like David did. Put on the cloak of zeal and take down every Goliath in your life. I am your victory banner.

ISAIAH 59:17; 2 TIMOTHY 1:6; 1 SAMUEL 30:6

PRAYER

Father, adorn me with Your cloak of zeal and give me a sense of urgency about the enemy's work against me. Help me stay alert and stirred up in my spirit.

DECREE

I decree the enemy's fervor against me is no match for the favor of God that rests upon me. I declare zeal for God's house consumes me, in Jesus's name.

June 2

Believe My Promises of Provision

*Y*ou call Me the God of more than enough. But when lack comes knocking at your door, you answer. You've heard Me tell you that I will supply all your needs. But when the voice of lack tells you that you won't have enough, you seem to forget who I am. Deliver yourself from the fear of lack and from lack attacks by meditating on My love. If your heavenly Father gave you His Son, what more would I not give you. Instead of walking in fear, walk with a heart of thanksgiving that I am not a man that I should lie. I promised you provision. Believe Me.

Exodus 16:17–18; 1 Kings 17:14–16; Psalm 34:9

PRAYER

Father, forgive me for ever doubting you as my provider. Help me truly repent—to change the way I think about Kingdom economy so I can receive Your provision.

DECREE

I decree lack attacks cannot stand up against the outpouring of provision in my life. I declare the voice of lack has no audience with me, in Jesus's name.

Avoid Demonic Connections

You've heard of divine connections. These are the connections that propel your life forward. Look for them. Appreciate them. Guard them. But beware of the counterfeits. The enemy works to counterfeit what is divine. A fleshly or demonic connection can at first look divine. These counterfeit connections make promises, flatter you, and otherwise work to get close to you but their motive is not divine—it's fleshly or demonic. Don't operate in suspicion but don't take everything at face value. Don't ignore the check I will give you in your spirit when a counterfeit connection arises. I am trying to protect you. I have someone better for you.

1 CORINTHIANS 15:33; PROVERBS 27:6; PROVERBS 18:24

PRAYER

Father, I need greater discernment. Help me navigate the realm of relationships and quickly determine by Your Spirit who You've sent to walk with me and who is against me.

DECREE

I decree demonic connections the enemy sends to thwart my life are found out and pruned. I declare divine connections are in my present and future, in Jesus's name.

June 4

Press In to See

$\mathcal{D}$on't allow the enemy to cause you to see through a glass darkly those things I am trying to show you plainly. Determine to come up higher through the persistence of your will to study My Word and press into My presence. Don't be satisfied with seeing through the glass darkly. Don't be satisfied with knowing in part and seeing in part and moving in part when I am speaking expressly to your heart. Press in for the part that you have not seen—the part the enemy does not want you to see. Press in. Press in. Press in. Press in. Press in. Press in.

PSALM 119:18; PROVERBS 15:3; 1 CHRONICLES 16:11

PRAYER

Father, help me see what You want me to see when You want me to see it. Give me a determined heart to press past my natural sight into the unseen realm. Open my eyes.

DECREE

I decree the enemy's attempts to blind my spiritual eyes are canceled. I declare the eyes of my heart are open wide and I see what eyes cannot see, in Jesus's name.

June 5

Decree Peace to the Storm

*B*e at peace and then decree peace to the storm that's raging against your life. Become the peace you want to see in your life. Determine in your heart you will walk in your shoes of peace—the peace that passes all understanding. Determine peace is part of your armor and use it to guard your heart, even when the enemy is working overtime to bring turmoil into your soul. The Prince of Peace has bestowed His peace upon you. Peace is part of your spiritual inheritance. Don't let go of it.

MARK 4:39; JOHN 14:27; 2 THESSALONIANS 3:16

PRAYER

Father, let Your peace envelop me continually as I pursue Your heart. Help me never to forsake peace even when it feels like the storm is pushing me out of Your promises.

DECREE

I decree peace to the demonic storms raging against my life, and I forbid storms from forming over my life. I declare I walk in the supernatural peace of God, in Jesus's name.

Who Do You Need to Forgive?

$\mathscr{I}$ve told you in My Word and illustrated time and time again the power of forgiveness. Refusing to forgive opens the door to the enemy. You've been forgiven of so much. I continue to forgive you. When you refuse to return this mercy on those who have wronged you—when you determine to hold a grudge—you are inviting the tormenters to wreak havoc on your mind. You are inviting demon powers to harass you. You are welcoming hindering spirits to thwart you. Who do you need to forgive?

MATTHEW 6:14–15; MARK 11:25; LUKE 17:3–4

PRAYER

Father, I choose by force of my will to forgive all those in my past and present who have abused me or accused me in any way. Give me the grace of forgiveness.

DECREE

I decree the agenda of unforgiveness is crippled, obstructed, and interrupted in my life. I declare forgiveness flows freely from my heart like a river, in Jesus's name.

Let Your Spirit Take the Lead

The enemy had no place in Jesus. Although He was tempted, He was sinless. He did not have a sin nature like yours. Your flesh is at enmity with Me. Your flesh wars against My Spirit. Crucify your flesh and its lusts so the enemy has less in you to work with. For although there is no good thing in your flesh, you can choose to allow your spirit to lead the charge. You don't have to follow the desires of the flesh. Your will and your spirit in line with My Spirit guarantee victory.

GALATIANS 5:17–18; COLOSSIANS 1:10–11; JOHN 15:4

PRAYER

Father, I surrender my will to Your will. Help me reject the desires of the flesh, which is weak because of my carnal nature. Remember my frame and that I am but dust.

DECREE

I decree false spirits trying to seduce me are frustrated and inhibited. I declare my inner man is stronger than my outer man because it is being renewed day by day, in Jesus's name.

Rejoice Now in Your Victory

I, Myself, will bring you through to the other side of this lengthy battle. You will have joy and you will have laughter and you will have peace that passes all understanding. You will walk with Me in a new dimension of compassion. You will see others around you who are hurting like you once were, like you even are now, and you will stop for the one and you will say, "How can I help? How can I pray?" because you'll remember how you had to walk through alone where no man helped you; only My Spirit was there to console you. I will do it.

1 Samuel 2:1; Philippians 3:4; Psalm 33:1

PRAYER

Father, help me encourage myself in Your presence, Your victory, and Your peace. Help me hold on to Your mighty right hand as You lead me through the fire.

DECREE

I decree I am an agent of God's healing power in my generation. I declare My God is a very present help in time of need, in Jesus's name.

June 9

Get Off the Ferris Wheel of Emotions

ℛise up now and begin to fight for your restoration. Begin to fight against the thoughts. Begin to fight against the emotions. Get off the Ferris wheel of your up and down feelings. Stop climbing down the ladder that descends into the pits of sorrow and depression and grief. Begin instead to climb a ladder toward Heaven. Rise up and ascend. Climb higher in My Spirit because there is a safe place under the shadow of My wings, where everything fades away and you can see clearly again.

JOB 15:12; PROVERBS 15:13; PROVERBS 15:28

PRAYER

Father, help me stay steady when the world around me seems to be spinning out of control. Help me stay focused on You so You can keep Your promise to keep me in perfect peace.

DECREE

I decree sevenfold restoration in every area the enemy has struck my life. I declare I am ascending in the spirit where I can see more like God, in Jesus's name.

Stand in My Winner's Circle

I always lead you into the victorious place—into the winner's circle. My winner's circle isn't so small that it's only big enough for you. My winner's circle has room enough for every single one of My sons and daughters. I've called you all to stand in the winner's circle with arms lifted up in victory. Don't allow the enemy to pull you into strife and competition. Instead of competing with your brother and competing with your sister and even competing with yourself, begin to cooperate with My Spirit. My winner's circle is big enough for all of you. I don't shun anybody, and I don't shut anybody out.

1 John 5:4–5; Philippians 2:3; 2 Timothy 2:5

PRAYER

Father, thank You for always making me a winner. I lift up my hands even now in victory and praise to the God of my triumph. Help me avoid the trap of competition.

DECREE

I decree spirits of jealousy and envy working to derail my victory are decimated. I declare I walk with a cooperative spirit with my brothers and sisters for the glory of Christ, in Jesus's name.

June 11

The Enemy Will Not Get an Advantage Over You

*Y*ou will soon see the results of the refining fire that marked your life in the past season. The enemy took advantage of you during the trial, but you're coming out like precious silver and gold. I brought up the impurities in your soul, so I purify you. I have made room to pour more of Myself into you. I've positioned you for new glory. The fire you walked through burned up impure motives and things that hindered love. It burned up things I never put in you and things that don't belong in you. I've burned them up, so you don't burn out as you make another push into My will for you.

ZECHARIAH 13:9; 1 PETER 1:7; PROVERBS 17:3

PRAYER

Father, the fire is so hot and sometimes it burns. Help me to trust You in the refining process so I can shine like gold in a dark world.

DECREE

I decree the fire of God burns up the enemy's agenda. I declare that same fire is burning away everything in my life that hinders my next glory in Christ, in Jesus's name.

June 12

My Power Is Backing You in the Battle

Understand and know that My power is backing you in the battle. My heavenly host is backing you in the war. My grace rests upon you in the weariness. My anointing flows through you in your moment of need. Move forward with the sword of the Spirit in your hand and recover those things the enemy ripped from your hands. As you wait on Me for instruction, I will cause you to look down upon your enemies and see their strategies before they are fully executed so that you can combat them with My Word.

ACTS 1:8; EPHESIANS 3:20; ISAIAH 40:29

PRAYER

Father, thank You for seating me in heavenly places with Christ Jesus so I can look down on the enemy and laugh the way You do. Help me see what You see.

DECREE

I decree the spirit of might enables me to overpower my spiritual foes. I declare God's power flows through my veins and from my belly, in Jesus's name.

I Will Not Allow the Enemy to Harm You

Stop trying to figure it all out. Stop ruminating. Stop worrying. Stop meditating on the negative, and begin to meditate on who I am. For I am your light, and I am your salvation. I am the lifter of your head and the lover of your soul. I am the One who created you, and I am the One who sustains your life. And I will not let one hair on your head be harmed. You can trample on serpents and scorpions and nothing shall by any means harm you. Believe it!

PROVERBS 12:25; MATTHEW 6:27; LUKE 10:19

PRAYER

Father, help me become more self-aware of my thoughts and the intentions of my heart. Spur me to meditate on the Word so my mind is renewed little by little.

DECREE

I decree the Word of God in my mouth worries worrying spirits that work to worry and weary me. I declare my mouth speaks forth faith words, which shield me from harm, in Jesus's name.

You Will Conquer All

*W*hen you sustain an enemy hit, you may feel like you can't see through the tears. You may feel like you can't see through the witchcraft. You may feel like you can't see the forest from the trees, but I'm in the thick of it. I haven't left you. I will wipe away every tear, and you will conquer every enemy. When you walk with Me, I will make a way. I am the way. So, look for Me through the tears, and look for Me through the witchcraft, and look for Me because I am still with you. You will conquer all.

ROMANS 8:37; REVELATION 12:11; JOHN 14:6

PRAYER

Father, help me navigate the realm of emotions versus the realm of the spirit so I know when my tears are emotional and when they are travail.

DECREE

I decree witchcraft coming at me is returned to the sender with interest. I declare God collects every single one of my tears in a bottle and answers my cries for deliverance, in Jesus's name.

Forgive Yourself

*J*esus took on your guilt at the cross. You don't have to walk with the heavy weight of unquenchable guilt when you disappoint people or when you disappoint Me. The enemy is quick to heap guilt on your soul to cripple you so that you can't run to the throne for a shower in My love and cleansing by the blood of Jesus. When you hurt someone, when you disobey My Word, when you choose not to do what you know is right, or when you make an accidental mistake that causes trouble, punishing yourself makes you vulnerable to more enemy attack. Seek forgiveness. Forgive yourself, and shut out the enemy.

1 John 1:9; Romans 5:1; Psalm 103:11–12

PRAYER

Father, remind me to run to the throne room and obtain grace and mercy to help me stay anchored in Your Word when guilt and disappointment are screaming at me.

DECREE

I decree spirits of guilt, shame, and every dark force working to cripple my walk in Christ is incapacitated and disappointed. I declare love covers a multitude of sins, in Jesus's name.

June 16

I Am Shaking Up Your Paradigm

I am shaking up your paradigm of who I am and who you are in Me. I am shaking and stirring your perception of who the enemy is and who he is not. For at times you see the enemy as greater than, bigger than, stronger than. But you need to see Me as all of that and more. I am greater than. I am bigger than. I am stronger than, and I am on the inside of you. So, open your eyes and take another look. Open your eyes, and I will remove the scales that have caused you to see in part, to know in part, and to walk in partial blindness.

1 JOHN 4:4; ZEPHANIAH 3:17; PSALM 147:5

PRAYER

Father, open the eyes of my heart so I can see You for who You are. Purge me of inaccurate perspectives of You, Your character, and Your love.

DECREE

I decree a shaking to the enemy's evil hierarchy of darkness. I declare I am strong in Him and the power of His might, in Jesus's name.

Testify to My Vindicating Power

When you come through the other side of this, I will strengthen you to minister to others. You will remind them of who I am in the midst of their fiery trial. You will tell them your testimony. You will tell them how the enemy shook you to your core, then you will tell them how I stepped in. You will tell them how I grabbed hold of you, made you able to stand, gave you strength for the battle, vindicated you, and took vengeance upon your enemy. You will testify of My goodness.

ISAIAH 43:2; PSALM 27:3; PSALM 66:16

PRAYER

Father, I will sing of Your love forever. I will testify to Your goodness and mercy. Put a new song in my heart, and I will praise you with my mouth.

DECREE

I decree my testimony sets people free. I declare the goodness of the Lord in the land of the living marks my life in every season, in Jesus's name.

Take a Deep Breath

*W*hatever comes against you, remember I am for you and with you. My favor surrounds you like a shield. Remember, whatever tries to come to knock the wind out of you, I've put my breath on the inside of you. My *pneuma* life is blowing over you. My *zoe* life dwells on the inside of you. The Spirit that raised Christ from the dead has taken up residence in you. Resurrection power is sustaining you. Take a deep breath.

PSALM 5:8; JOB 33:4; ISAIAH 11:2

PRAYER

Father, when I feel breathless, please blow Your wind over me so I can feel the refreshing of Your Spirit. Let Your wind carry me above the attack.

DECREE

I decree the breathlessness upon the enemy that tried to knock the wind out of my lungs. I declare I see and skirt the fiery darts of the wicked one, in Jesus's name.

Abolishing the Cloud of Injustice

I want to abolish the cloud of injustice, and I want My glory cloud to follow you. I want you to walk in My glory, but you must forgive those who wronged you. You must forgive those who just did you dirty. You must forgive those who put the knife in your back and then weren't content to leave it there but had to twist it around a few times to inflict more pain. You must be willing to forgive in order to receive My justice. As long as you want to let the enemy drag you around with feelings of bitterness, you will not receive the fullness of My justice and My vengeance and My vindication. So, continue to surge against injustice but do so with clean hands.

ECCLESIASTES 3:17; PSALM 101:1; HOSEA 12:6

PRAYER

Father, pull the knife of betrayal out of my back and heal the wounds of my heart. Bring justice to my life. I choose to forgive those who hurt me. Vindicate me, oh Lord.

DECREE

I decree justice over the wicked operations of my spiritual foes. I declare vengeance belongs to the Lord, so I will wait upon Him with a forgiving heart, in Jesus's name.

June 20

I Am a Tactical God

Try a new way. Try a new thing. The old ways you've executed spiritual warfare aren't working in this new battle because it's not the right strategy. The old strategy isn't taking you over the top to victory because it's not My specific way for this battle. Seek My strategy, and I will show you a new way. I will show you how to get over, past, around and breakthrough the spiritual opposition that is frustrating you. Don't leave Me out of your battle plans. I have all the answers. I am a tactical God.

2 CORINTHIANS 5:17; ISAIAH 42:10; EPHESIANS 6:11

PRAYER

Father, give me Your battle plan for every war you send me to fight. Help me wait on Your directions, Your strategies, and Your tactics for victory.

DECREE

I decree my enemies shall not triumph over me but shall trip and fall over their own feet. I declare my God has already paved the way for resounding victory in the fight, in Jesus's name.

Prophesy Back to the Devil

The enemy loves to prophesy lies to your soul. Prophesy back to the devil. Consider how Goliath prophesied to David. The giant prophesied David's fate was death. David did not run from the battle line in fear and trembling. David prophesied back to the enemy. David prophesied the fate of the devil that would dare to come against his God. David knew My voice and My will. So do you. Prophesy My will to the enemy that's prophesying lies to your soul.

2 PETER 1:20–21; PROVERBS 18:21; PSALM 103:20

PRAYER

Father, give me an unction to function in the prophetic realms of warfare. Help me see with my spiritual eyes what the enemy is doing and counter it with Your Word.

DECREE

I decree the enemy's false prophecies over my life fall to the ground and die. I declare my mouth prophesies the unwavering will of the Lord all my days, in Jesus's name.

Check Your Heart

*W*hen you find yourself in a fiery trial and when you find yourself in the fiery furnace of affliction, check your heart. I am not sending the trial, and I am not sending the warfare, but if you have given the enemy something to work with, he will work with it. If you have common ground with the enemy of your soul, his voice many deceive you. You may think what you are hearing are your thoughts. Examine yourself. Renounce your sin. Break agreement with the wicked one. Repentance is a gift.

ISAIAH 48:10; 2 CORINTHIANS 13:5; 1 PETER 1:10–11

PRAYER

Father, examine my heart and see if You find any wicked way in me. Help me see the sinful tendencies in my life that are inviting the enemy to wreak havoc on my soul.

DECREE

I decree the enemy's unfair advantage ceases because the power of repentance blocks his access. I declare God is renewing my mind by His Word, in Jesus's name.

I Will Shield You From the Fire

The enemy works to sideline you—or convince you to sideline yourself. The enemy works to blindside you—or blind you with lies. The enemy works through people to release so-called friendly fire against you. Sometimes the attack comes from all sides. Sometimes people who were supposed to stand with you and for you stand against you, and the pain is so great you can hardly stand. Take heart. I will open your eyes and show you things to come. I will shield you from the fiery darts when you run to me. I am the strength of your life. I will heal your pain and make you stand.

1 John 5:18; Psalm 91:4; Psalm 84:11

PRAYER

Father, shield me from enemy fire, and I will be shielded. Strengthen me to stand and withstand when my Christian brothers and sisters rise up against me.

DECREE

I decree the enemy's sinister plots to sideline me with unforgiveness are suspended. I declare my heart is postured to bless, release, and forgive, in Jesus's name.

I Am Laughing at Your Enemies

I am on your side. I am the captain of the host. No one can come against Me, and although they come against you, I am for you and with you. I sit in the Heavens, and I laugh at my enemies. I'm laughing at your enemies because I see their end and I see your end. The devil's end is destruction. The spirits that attack you will land in the lake of fire. Their end is eternal torment. But your latter shall be greater than your past. Your end is victory. Your end breakthrough. Your end is eternal life. Keep your mind set on things above. Laugh at your enemies.

PSALM 37:13; PSALM 2:4; 1 CHRONICLES 16:35

PRAYER

Father, help me to laugh with You when I feel like crying under the pressure of enemy attack. Help me see the irony in the enemy's prideful onslaught against me.

DECREE

I decree the eternal fate of my foes is sealed. I declare my portion in this battle is to rejoice in the Lord's victory on the cross and my right standing with Him, in Jesus's name.

June 25

Don't Fall for the Enemy's Shock and Awe Attack

Keep your eyes on the prize. Don't be shocked and don't be dismayed by the shock and awe of the enemy. Don't be overwhelmed by the stall tactics that keep your promises out of reach. Understand and know that I have the ultimate shock and awe plan. I will shock the enemy who is prideful and who is wicked. I will shock the enemy who thinks he has it all figured out. The wicked one knows his days are numbered. That's why he is raging against you with shocking trials. Don't be in awe of the enemy's attack. Stay in awe of Me. Keep standing and know that I am strengthening you. I am holding you up. I am your shield and buckler.

PSALM 55:2–3; NUMBERS 10:9; PSALM 92:10–11

PRAYER

Father, help me execute Your shock and awe plan against the enemy's camp. Help me see through the subterfuge of the wicked one into the triumph You've given me.

DECREE

I decree shock and dismay overtake every enemy working against my life. I declare I walk in continuous awe of the one true, living God, in Jesus's name.

Push Harder Than You've Ever Pushed Before

I am making up for lost time in your life. Everything will shift and everything will change as you let go of the victim mentality and adopt a conqueror's mentality. I know how disappointing it is for you when things you were supposed to birth did not come to a head because the enemy thwarted you. I am going to make up for lost time with multiple births in this next season as you determine to push and push harder than you've ever pushed before. The battle will not get easier, but My grace is sufficient.

JOEL 2:25; ROMANS 8:11; 2 PETER 3:9

PRAYER

Father, thank You for redeeming the time. Help me do my part to push and keep on pushing until the enemy is out of the way of Your will for my life.

DECREE

I decree the plans of every enemy that has thwarted me and caused me delays are consumed by holy fire. I declare darkness is giving way to God's light, in Jesus's name.

I Have Not Stationed Opposition Against You

Rise up and break the word curses people are releasing over your life. Rise up and break the assignments of the enemy brewing in the spirit. Rise up and break the opposition. I've not stationed the opposition against you, but I've stationed you to overcome. I've called you more than a conqueror. I've called you an overcomer, and I've called you a winner. I've stamped and marked you as one who presses through and who comes out the other side with arms raised to praise My name. Rise up!

PROVERBS 26:2; PROVERBS 15:4; HEBREWS 12:1

PRAYER

Father, give me the strength in my inner man to oppose the opposition to my breakthrough. Help me press and keep on pressing until I see the victory.

DECREE

I decree the enemy brewing evil works for my life is drowned in his own stew. I declare God has marked me for consistent breakthrough, in Jesus's name.

June 28

When the Enemy Works to Pressurize You

*O*ne of the enemy's strategies is to pressurize you. He wants to keep the heat on with circumstantial pressure, spiritual pressure, physical pressure, and financial pressure. He wants you to feel under pressure like a kettle about to blow its top. When you feel pressurized—when you discern the enemy is trying to force your hand with his pressure tactics and coerce you into bad decisions—take a deep breath. Breathe of My peace. Breathe in My love. Breathe and wait on Me. I will alleviate your pressure as you press into My presence. That is your anti-pressure strategy.

JAMES 1:12; 1 CORINTHIANS 1:10; 1 PETER 1:6–7

PRAYER

Father, help me withstand the pressure that makes me feel like I am going to blow my top. Help me maintain a cool spirit so my adversary doesn't see me sweat.

DECREE

I decree enemies that are pressing me on every side bow to the pressure of the Word of God in my mouth. I declare I persevere through demonic pressure, in Jesus's name.

Reverse the Enemy's Lies

*W*hen the enemy breathes lies—when the lies are coming fast and furious—take a hint. The enemy works in deception. You know he is the father of lies and has been lying since the beginning. But you also need to recognize this: the enemy is lying against the truth. Many times the enemy's lies can point you to My truth if you'll just flip the script. When the enemy tells you that you can't pay your bills, know that a financial breakthrough will come as you sow in faith and trust Me. Reverse the enemy's lies, and you'll discover the truth that will set you free from oppression.

PROVERBS 16:9; PSALM 27:12; PSALM 25:5

PRAYER

Father, help me discern when the enemy is twisting Your Word and lying against the truth. Keep me from falling into the snare of the enemy trying to deceive my soul.

DECREE

I decree the enemy is ensnared by the truth of God's Word that reveals his lies. I declare every lie of the enemy is reversed and God's truth prevails in my heart, in Jesus's name.

June 30

When You've Been Worn Down and Torn Down

I know some situations you face seem too difficult for you in this season because you've been worn down and torn down. Take heart. Nothing is too hard for Me. I am breathing new life upon you, and I am building you up. So, don't say, "I cannot go forward." Don't say, "I cannot take another step." Don't say, "No one understands," because I, Myself, understand. Jesus is the high priest who understands. Jesus is the high priest of your confession. I am your intercessor. I am your standby. I am with you.

HEBREWS 3:1; HEBREWS 7:25; JOHN 14:26

PRAYER

Father, help me recover from enemy tactics to wear me down and tear me down. Restore my soul in the aftermath of the spiritual war and help me rise again.

DECREE

I decree the spirit of weariness attacking my life is worn out and fails to overcome me. I declare my Redeemer lives and He is redeeming my soul day by day, in Jesus's name.

JULY

Be sober, be vigilant; because your adversary the devil walks about like a roaring lion, seeking whom he may devour. Resist him, steadfast in the faith, knowing that the same sufferings are experienced by your brotherhood in the world. But may the God of all grace, who called us to His eternal glory by Christ Jesus, after you have suffered a while, perfect, establish, strengthen, and settle you.

1 PETER 5:8–10

July 1

The Enemy Doesn't Need an Open Door

The enemy doesn't need a wide open door to attack you. The enemy doesn't need you to leave your door unlocked in order to gain entrance into your life. Satan attacked Jesus in the wilderness with temptations, didn't he? Satan attacked Jesus's mind in the Garden of Gethsemane at a low point of His life, didn't he? The scribes and Pharisees attacked Jesus constantly, didn't they? Judas betrayed Him, didn't he? Jesus was sinless, but He suffered attacks. Check for open doors and sinful behavior but know the enemy can strike at opportune times. Stay alert.

MATTHEW 4:1–11; MATTHEW 26:46–50; MARK 13:37

PRAYER

Father, help me not sleep or slumber but to watch and pray. Energize me to stay alert in the spirit so I can catch the thief before he strikes my household.

DECREE

I decree every open door in my life is slammed shut in the devil's face as I repent before the Lord. I declare I am watchful at all times, in Jesus's name.

July 2

You Won't Lose if You Give

The enemy wants to tell you that you'll lose more if you give more. But the opposite is true. There is grace for giving. There is grace for receiving. It's more blessed to give than to receive. I am able to make all grace abound toward you when you give. You will reap what you sow. There is a harvest for you—an abundant harvest that more than meets your every need. Don't let the enemy talk you out of the abundant harvest that I have ordained for you. You can't lose when you give.

ACTS 20:35; 2 CORINTHIANS 9:8; LUKE 12:33–34

PRAYER

Father, help me root out the little foxes that are spoiling my financial vine. Help me believe the truth—Your truth—about money, sowing, reaping, and spending.

DECREE

I decree grace for giving overwhelms and overflows in my life. I declare I receive from God, in good measure, pressed down, shaken together, and running over, in Jesus's name.

War and Worship Like David

*W*hen you face warfare like David did, look to Me like David did. Get into My Word. Read the Psalms of David. Read these passages of My Scripture that I left there to comfort generations. For just as David cried out for My comfort and I answered him, I will answer you. Just as David cried out for My protection from Saul and the Philistines, the enemies of his soul, I will protect you in the same way when you cry out to Me. I have surrounded you with a shield, and nothing shall by any means harm you.

PSALM 144:1; PSALM 27; PSALM 5:10

PRAYER

Father, give me a worshipping and warring anointing like David carried onto the battlefield. Remind me to cry out to You in my distress for swift deliverance.

DECREE

I decree the arms of my spiritual foes are broken and their grip is loosened on my soul. I declare my strong God delivers me from death and fear, in Jesus's name.

July 4

Enforce Your Freedom

When the chords of death seem to be encircling you and the pains of demonic powers feel like they are going to overtake you, cry out to Me. I will not let you fall. Cry out for strength to stand and withstand. Cry out for strategies and insight into the source of your attack. Cry out for freedom and deliverance. But don't stop there. Remember I have given you authority. After I give you strength, strategies, and insight, take your authority and walk into the freedom and deliverance that Jesus paid the price to give you. Enforce your freedom.

PSALM 116:3–6; PSALM 143; PSALM 49

PRAYER

Father, I lift up my voice to You and You alone. Give me strategies and insights, tactics and devices to break through the enemy's plans to bind me in chains.

DECREE

I decree I walk in divine wisdom for victorious warfare. I declare God has given me authority over all the power of the enemy and nothing shall by any means harm me, in Jesus's name.

Get Refreshed for the Showdown

*W*hen you feel like you can't carry your sword and shield anymore, come away with Me. Come and hide under the shadow of My wings where there is safety and peace and rest for your weary soul. Even though you'll still have to deal with the warfare when you emerge from My loving shadow, you'll emerge with renewed strength and power and might. You'll be ready to face again those demons from your past that keep on coming back around at particularly inconvenient seasons to stop you from breaking through in different areas of your life.

MATTHEW 11:28; ACTS 3:20–21; EXODUS 33:14

PRAYER

Father, give me rest for my soul that is weary from the battle. Strengthen my aching arms and my feeble knees from this lengthy war.

DECREE

I decree demon powers emerge in inconvenient seasons are detoured and rerouted to dry places. I declare I will enter into the rest of my God even in the fiercest battle, in Jesus's name.

Sabotage the Spirit of Sabotage

The spirit of sabotage is skilled in bringing destruction to your life. Sabotage is a patient enemy. Sabotage is sneakier than other demons that operate to kill, steal, and destroy your life. Sabotage doesn't have a loud voice, and it doesn't make a lot of noise. It's stealth. But you can unmask it. You can discern it. You can overcome it. You can sabotage the spirit of sabotage by being vigilant in the spirit. Keep your eyes wide open. Watch and pray.

ISAIAH 5:20–21; GENESIS 3:1–21; MATTHEW 26:41

PRAYER

Father, help me discern the subtle operations of sabotaging spirits that seek to bring wreckage to my best-laid plans. Unmask this nefarious spirit.

DECREE

I decree the spirit of sabotage attacking my life is sabotaged by the Spirit of God. I declare I walk in the clear path the Lord has set forth for me, in Jesus's name.

July 7

Jesus Is Stronger Than Jezebel

Jezebel is spoken of with such reverence. Don't be ignorant to this devil's devices, but don't glorify this principality in your midst. You can resist the maneuvers of Jezebel when you break agreement with it. Jesus rebuked the church at Thyatira for tolerating Jezebel. You can't break a Jezebel assignment if you have a Jezebel alignment. Stop allowing this spirit to manipulate you, to control you, to seduce you, and otherwise wreak havoc on your life. Take your stand. Jesus is more powerful than Jezebel. Never forget it.

REVELATION 2:20; 1 CORINTHIANS 15:33; PSALM 12:2

PRAYER

Father, help me break any and all Jezebelic alignments in my life. Give me an intolerance and a righteous indignation regarding the Jezebel spirit.

DECREE

I decree flattering lips are bound together in my presence. I declare Jezebel's seduction has no power over me because my love for God guards my heart, in Jesus's name.

Pop the Devil's Hot Air Balloon

The enemy is full of hot air. He huffs and he puffs, hoping to blow your house down. He makes a lot of noise to get your attention. He breathes lies. It's time to pop the devil's balloon. It's time to deflate his strategy against your mind. It's time to pierce the enemy's darkness with the light of My Word. When you feel the enemy's hot air at the back of your neck, turn around and speak the truth. Speak My Word with authority. Release blowback against the enemy's hot air. He may talk a lot, but you don't have to listen to the lies.

2 CORINTHIANS 10:5; 1 PETER 5:8; 2 CORINTHIANS 11:3

PRAYER

Father, help me resist the temptation to run and hide when I feel the enemy's heat on my soul. Remind me in that moment of who I am in Christ and the authority I carry.

DECREE

I decree the devil's hot air evaporates in God's glorious presence around my life. I declare I live, move, and have my being in God's presence and no foe can stand against me, in Jesus's name.

War From a Position of Victory

*P*ush back the darkness now. Purge the Heavens over your life with words of life. You are seated in Christ in heavenly places, so war from a position of victory. Stop tolerating the work of the enemy in your life. I've given you the authority to stop it. I've given you the keys to the Kingdom. You determine what you let in your mind and in your heart. The entrance of My Word brings light and life. The entrance of the wicked one's words brings darkness and death. Push out the darkness. Deliver yourself from darkness by renewing your mind with the light of My Word. Your legal position is victory. Walk in it.

EPHESIANS 2:6; MATTHEW 16:19; JOHN 1:5

PRAYER

Father, You are light, and You are love. Help me to put on Christ, to walk with Him, even as I am seated with Him in heavenly places. Teach me to leverage Your authority.

DECREE

I decree a death sentence on the enemy's plans to move me off the position of victory. I declare my heart is strong and my mind is fixed on the Lord, in Jesus's name.

Don't You Think I Have a Plan?

Don't you think I have a plan? Yes, indeed, I do have a plan for you that exceeds anything you could ever ask for or imagine. Don't give up just shy of the breakthrough. Don't stop praying. Don't stop pushing. If you could just see what I see instead of what the enemy is showing you, you would put your mouth in line with My Word. If you could just look beyond the enemy's smoke and mirrors, you would rejoice. You would dance. You would shout. You would leap. You would call and tell all your friends of My goodness. So, look by faith and rejoice because the enemy cannot stop My plans for you unless you let him. Don't let him.

JEREMIAH 29:11; PSALM 33:11; PSALM 5:11

PRAYER

Father, would You give me a glimpse of the plans you have hidden from the enemy? Would you let me peek at what's next so I can prepare for the battle against it?

DECREE

I decree the warfare against God's plan for my life ricochets back to the enemy. I declare God's plans are higher than my plans—and they are good, in Jesus's name.

Attacked on Two Fronts

*W*hen your body is under attack, know this: your mind is also under attack. Every attack against you, whether it's against your family, your body, your finances, your career, every attack against you comes with a mind battle on top of it. For you are battling to believe My Word over the wicked one's lies. You are battling to believe what you can't see is true in the face of what you can see—the sickness, the lack, the relational woes. Gird up the loins of your mind because when you win the battle there, the enemy will exit these other areas of your life.

ROMANS 10:17; HEBREWS 1:11; 1 CORINTHIANS 2:5

PRAYER

Father, help me see clearly the two-pronged attacks of the enemy and fight them on both fronts. Help me gird up my mind so I can keep the enemy out of my heart.

DECREE

I decree when the enemy comes at me two ways, he has to flee fourteen ways. I declare when the enemy is caught stealing, he repays seven times, in Jesus's name.

July 12

You Will Surely See a Great Reward

What if I told you every failure was a success in disguise? What if I told you every loss was a win in the waiting? What if I told you everything stolen from your hand would be repaid with interest? Look at every failure, loss, and theft at the hand of the enemy through the eyes of eternity and rejoice. Don't let the losses, the betrayals, and the pain make you bitter. Let it push You deeper into My presence. Trust Me. If you don't see full vindication on this side of Heaven, you will surely see a great reward in the age to come. Trust Me.

PSALM 91:2; HEBREWS 10:36; PSALM 62:8

PRAYER

Father, help me see the way You see. Give me the ability to see the opposite of what the enemy wants me to look at and focus on Your ability to turn it all around.

DECREE

I decree the enemy of my reward is jilted and denied, but I am vindicated and victorious. I declare my everlasting trust in the everlasting God who never fails, in Jesus's name.

I Am the Light at the End of the Tunnel

I've seen your trials, and I've seen the tragic circumstances work to overtake you. I know it seems like it will never end. But I not only see the light at the end of the tunnel, I am the light at the end of the tunnel. I am the light that illuminates your path to victory. I am the way, and I am the truth, and I am the life, and I am the light of the world. I am living on the inside of you, and I will illuminate your mind. I will pour wisdom upon you liberally when you ask. So, don't concentrate on the tragic circumstances that cloud your mind with darkness. Focus on the light. Focus on Me. I will lead you through.

JOHN 8:12; 2 CORINTHIANS 4:6; ISAIAH 9:2

PRAYER

Father, You see all things and know all things. You know the way to go and how far to take me. Help me follow Your leadership in all my ways.

DECREE

I decree darkness flees in the presence of my light. I declare I see clearly because the Word of God is a lamp unto my feet and a light unto my path, in Jesus's name.

Past Defeats Do Not Define Your Future

When a new day dawns, don't dwell on the attacks of yesterday. Don't look back to the defeats of the day before. But look up. Look to Me. I am your victory banner. Every day is new. The attacks and apparent defeats of the past do not define your future. The enemy wants to hold you in fear, anticipating his next move and method of combat. But I have not given you a spirit of fear. I have given you My power and authority. So get back up again and resist the temptation to set your mind on the attacks and defeats. Set your mind on victory instead. Your victory is in Me.

PSALM 20:5; PSALM 56:3; PSALM 94:19

PRAYER

Father, help me to keep looking forward and moving forward, despite the losses of the past. Show me a better way. Strengthen me to resist thoughts of defeat.

DECREE

I decree my latter shall be greater than my past and my next victory sweeter than anything lost. I declare I walk in victory because I walk in Christ and He is my victory banner, in Jesus's name.

Nothing Can Shake You Free from My Hand

*Y*our faith in My Son gives you permission; it authorizes you to come boldly to Me and ask for what you need from Me and request mercy and receive grace from Me. I am here for you. Even though it seems like everything around you is shaking and everything on the inside of you is shaking, rest assured that nothing can shake you free from My hand. Nothing can shake you loose from My love because I am with you, and I will never leave you, and I will never forsake you even to the end of the age. I am with you and I am for you, and if I am for you, then who can be against you?

JOHN 10:28; HEBREWS 13:5; HEBREWS 12:28–29

PRAYER

Father, thank You for holding me tight and keeping me safe under the shadow of Your wings. Let me feel Your presence when the shaking overwhelms me.

DECREE

I decree satanic shaking in my life must settle in the presence of Yeshua. I declare the Lord looks on my affliction and my distress and rescues me, in Jesus's name.

The Enemy Can't Stop You

*Y*ou are unstoppable in Christ as you follow after My Spirit and obey My Word. The enemy can't stop you. Even if you stumble, I will grab your hand and pick you up and fortify your spirit. I will set you on your feet. I am able to make you stand against any enemy opposition. So, look upon me, the unstoppable God. Don't look at all the obstacles and challenges and let them intimidate you. Don't look at all the things that have gone wrong in the past. Don't let your circumstances speak death to you. Listen to My still, small voice. My voice carries life.

1 KINGS 19:11–12; ROMANS 8:31; PSALM 29:3

PRAYER

Father, help me look past the obstacles to the prize that You are calling me toward. Help me see past what is going wrong to the One who is always right.

DECREE

I decree every enemy that attempts to stop my assignment is barred, banned, and blocked. I declare my voice brings destruction to the enemy by the power of God's Word, in Jesus's name.

I Am Washing Your Eyes with Eye Salve

*F*or you have seen things one way in seasons past—you have seen things from the enemy's perspective—but I am washing your eyes with eye salve. You will begin to see things the way I see them. You will begin to see things that annoyed you, irritated you, and frustrated you will merely cause you to laugh at your enemies. You will walk in a place of freedom from the emotional reactions that caused you to walk in the flesh instead of My Spirit. You will see the enemy clearly and not be moved.

2 CORINTHIANS 5:7; 1 JOHN 5:20; 2 KINGS 6:17–20

PRAYER

Father, wash my eyes from disappointment and distress so I can see clearly where You are leading me. Strengthen me so I will be immovable in the face of attack.

DECREE

I decree the enemy's plans of destruction for my life are disappointed. I declare I operate in X-ray vision and see through the plots and plans of the enemy, in Jesus's name.

I Am Declaring Your Victory

I am the high priest of your confession, and I am not confessing defeat over you. I am declaring victory. I am your victory. I am not confessing feeling overwhelmed over you. I am confessing strength. I am your strength. I've already confessed it. I will confess it. I've rooted you and grounded you in My love. I've rooted you and grounded you in My wisdom. You have everything it takes to overcome because I am in you. I am the ultimate overcomer, and I've empowered you. You can do all things through Christ who strengthens you. Confess that.

DEUTERONOMY 20:4; PSALM 108:13; ROMANS 8:37

PRAYER

Father, help me to not merely confess Jesus as the high priest of my confession but to mind my mouth and mind my heart so I can confess Your Word in the warfare.

DECREE

I decree wisdom constrains my lips from uttering utter defeat. I declare breakthrough victory over my mind, my finances, my family, my health, and my everything, in Jesus's name.

July 19

When the Enemy Puts Pressure on Your Tongue

The enemy will put pressure on your tongue at every turn. You'll be tempted to speak out when you should stay silent. You'll be tempted to complain when you should be giving thanks. You'll be tempted to criticize when you should be edifying. Your tongue is an unruly evil, and it sets your life on hell. Don't let the enemy trick you and taunt you into speaking words of death and destruction. Use your words carefully, and when you are tempted to open your mouth wide for destruction, bite your tongue.

JAMES 3:8; EPHESIANS 4:29; PROVERBS 18:21

PRAYER

Father, strengthen my resolve to tame my tongue with Holy Spirit's help. Help me tap into the fruit of self-control to resist the temptations to speak out of line with your Word.

DECREE

I decree the enemy's cursing tongues turn back upon themselves. I declare that thanksgiving, praise, and edifying words emanate from my lips in obedience to God, in Jesus's name.

I Will Blow My Wind at Your Back

$\mathcal{R}$ise up again and begin to run again to face down your spiritual foes. I will blow My wind at your back, and you will outrun and outpace every enemy. You will put one foot in front of the other and race toward the assurance of victory. Those around and about you who want to see you fall and fail because of the jealousy in their hearts will be put to shame. Those who have spoken against you will have to admit that your God is the one true living God. You will outpace and you will outrun the enemies that try to tear you down and break you up. Rise up and run.

PSALM 30:1; EXODUS 23:22; PSALM 138:7

PRAYER

Father, give me boldness to rise up toe to toe with every foe who dares to challenge Your will for my life. Give me the courage to enforce Your statutes.

DECREE

I decree the wind of the Spirit is making a clean sweep of the enemy's residue from the past season of my life. I declare I will rise and run and win in this epic battle on earth, in Jesus's name.

Receive Strength to Take the Spoils

You've tasted bitter losses at the hand of the enemy, but you will see and taste and know that I am good as you sit in the presence of My Spirit Who comforts you. There is fullness of joy in My presence. You will gain strength for the next battle—strength to go to the enemy's camp and take back what he stole from you—as you let My joy strengthen you. I know the losses in the past season left you reeling, but the victories in the next season will make up for it and then some. Sit in My presence. Let Me restore your soul so you can fight again.

2 CHRONICLES 20:25; PSALM 16:11; PSALM 84:7

PRAYER

Father, strengthen me and I will be strengthened. Prepare me to outwit the enemy of my soul so I can maneuver past his schemes and gather the spoils.

DECREE

I decree double for my trouble and triple for my trial at the enemy's hand. I declare my mourning turns into dancing as I meditate on Your goodness, in Jesus's name.

July 22

I Will Keep Coming through for You

 am faithful. Even when the warfare is raging against your mind, I am faithful. Listen to Me. Get in My Word. Study My character. You will understand that I will come through for you again and again and again. I will keep on coming through for you. I will never let you down. I will never let you go. I will not relax My hold on you. The enemy cannot snatch you out of My hands. When you feel far away from Me, when you can't hear Me over the lies of the enemy, remember I am faithful. Learn of Me. I love you.

2 TIMOTHY 2:13; 1 CORINTHIANS 1:9; HEBREWS 10:23

PRAYER

Father, help me see how faithful You really are. Let me catch You being faithful over even the smallest things so that I will rest in Your faithfulness toward me.

DECREE

I decree the enemy's devices are set to self-destruct. I declare the goodness and the faithfulness of the Lord in the land of the living, in Jesus's name.

July 23

It's Only a Matter of Time

I will keep on propelling you forward to the degree that you let go of those things which lie behind. I will make you light as a feather. I will make you quick as a stallion. I will make you able and ready and willing in the day of My power to run to every battle line with fierce confidence knowing that it's only a matter of time before Goliath falls. It's only a matter of time before the wind shifts in your favor. It's only a matter of time before the dust settles. So, let go of the weights that slow you down and hold you down, and you will feel My winds of refreshing blow.

2 SAMUEL 22:30; GALATIANS 6:9; 2 CORINTHIANS 6:2

PRAYER

Father, help me trust in Your perfect timing for every aspect of my life, including overcoming the giants that have occupied what You have promised me.

DECREE

I decree the giant opposing me will lose his head to the sword of the Spirit. I declare my times are in God's hands, and my victory is secure and assured, in Jesus's name.

Walk Free from the Enemy's Torment

I saw the pain they inflicted upon your soul. I saw the rash judgments and the criticism against you. The enemy inspired them to turn on you, to pick on you, to wound you. But know this: When you rise up like Job and pray for those who used you, who abused you, and who spoke wrongly to you, you will find the healing balm of Gilead released into your heart. You will know and understand that the only One who matters is Me. What I say is all that matters. And I say you are lovely. I say you are strong. I say you are Mine. Pray for those who hurt you and walk free from the enemy's torment.

PSALM 56:9; PSALM 118:6–7; EZEKIEL 36:9

PRAYER

Father, I'm grateful You see all things, know all things, and have been with me through all things. Help me say about myself what You say even when I don't feel that way.

DECREE

I decree judgment over the evil forces opposing God's statutes and ordinances. I declare the torment with which the enemy has been tormenting me will turn upon him, in Jesus's name.

I Will Deliver You from the Taskmasters

I am your deliverer. I will deliver you from the snare of the fowler. I will deliver you from the habits that hold you back. I will deliver you from the ties that bind. I will deliver you from the raging war against your soul. I will deliver you from strongholds in your emotions. I will deliver you from pharaohs and taskmasters and injustices. I will redeem and restore. I will repay and reconcile. I will vindicate and bring you into victory as you press into My love.

ISAIAH 12:2; ISAIAH 45:15; MICAH 7:7

PRAYER

Father, thank You for total deliverance of my mind. Fill me again with Your Spirit so I can walk with you into the freedom You've called me to.

DECREE

I decree taskmasters do not master me but bow to the Jesus in me. I declare the spirit of Pharaoh working me to death will let me go so I can worship the Lord my God, in Jesus's name.

July 26

Refrain from Reacting to the Enemy's Plots

The enemy will continue to use the same tactics to kill, steal, and destroy until you stop reacting. When you react with fleshly anger, frustration, or any other way than My way, you are inviting more attacks. When the enemy of your soul sees what works against your mind, will, imaginations, reasonings, intellect, and emotions, he will keep attacking in that area. Respond by My Spirit instead of reacting out of your carnal nature and you'll stop the attack that's trying to stop you.

EPHESIANS 4:26; JAMES 4:7; 2 TIMOTHY 2:15

PRAYER

Father, help me to bite my tongue before I speak out of anger, frustration, or some other emotion that's tempting me to sin. Help me shut the devil up.

DECREE

I decree the devil's attempts to stir me up backfire in his face. I declare I walk in the peace of God so the devil doesn't see me sweat, in Jesus's name.

It's Never a Good Time for an Enemy Attack

It's never a good time for an enemy attack. Sometimes you think you could handle the warfare if the wicked one wasn't coming at you so many ways at once. But the reality is you're never going to feel like it's a good time for more attacks. So instead of complaining about the enemy's timing, take authority over the attack. Your times are in My hands, and you are in My grip. The attack may not come at a time you feel is convenient, but the enemy has come at what he has deemed an opportune time. Rise up and push back. You win.

LUKE 4:13; MATTHEW 28:18; 1 JOHN 4:4

PRAYER

Father, help me to stop complaining and start taking authority over the enemy that is pushing me to complain. Help me speak Your Word over my circumstances.

DECREE

I decree the enemy's untimely ambush recoils and traps him in his own net. I declare my authority over enemy powers works in every battle, in Jesus's name.

Jesus Will Never Let You Down

𝒯here is a friend who sticks closer than a brother, even in the warfare, and His name is Jesus. It's nice to have those around in about you who will fight with you and for you, but the reality is people will let you down. Jesus will never let you down. He will never leave you or forsake you in the middle of the battle. He will never leave you hanging with a dull sword and a rusty shield. When no one else will stand up for you, cry out to Jesus. He is your standby.

PROVERBS 18:24; PROVERBS 17:17; JOHN 1:1

PRAYER

Father, help me see Jesus as a Warrior, not just a Savior. Show me the King riding the white horse with vengeance against His enemies.

DECREE

I decree dullness to the enemy's sword and rust to his shield. I declare I overcome and overtake every demon power that challenges the warrior God in me, in Jesus's name.

You Will Beat Down the Mountains

I will make you a new sharp threshing instrument with teeth. You will not only speak to the mountains, you will thrush the mountains and beat them down with the words of your mouth. He will make the hills as chaff with the declarations and your proclamations and the prophecies you release into the atmosphere. I have given you an instrument of war called your tongue. Use it for good and not for evil. Use it to bind the works of darkness.

ISAIAH 41:5; JEREMIAH 51:20; JEREMIAH 50:25

PRAYER

Father, sharpen me and strengthen me, and I will serve as your battle-ax, your war club, your threshing instrument to tear down enemy opposition.

DECREE

I decree the weapons of God's indignation are active and at work in my spiritual war chest to decimate the wicked one's plans. I declare victory, in Jesus's name.

July 30

Don't Envy the Unjust

*D*on't worry and fear and complain because of the evil you see around and about you. Don't be jealous of people who seem to be getting ahead in a way that's unjust. You will see that those who are motivated by the flesh and those who are motivated by the enemy will not prosper. What looks like victory will turn into a loss for them. Stop looking at people and start looking at Me. I am the one who will give you lasting justice and lasting victory.

PSALM 37:1-11; ROMANS 12:9; PROVERBS 21:15

PRAYER

Father, the enemy tempts me to look at his handiwork, but help me keep my eyes on Your handiwork. Help me reject anger and wrath over evil spirits that work against me.

DECREE

I decree the devil's snare will catch his own foot and stop him dead in his tracks. I declare justice is my portion and payback is my future as I focus my heart on the Lord, in Jesus's name.

Don't Act Like the Enemy

*D*emons are subject to you in the name of Jesus. Understand and know the authority you carry and walk with a confidence in the midst of your spiritual foes and humility in the face of persecution from your enemies. You can't take authority over the enemy when you are acting like the enemy. Exercise your authority in dependence on Me, and you will overcome the wicked one.

PSALM 7:10; PSALM 62:7; EPHESIANS 4:27

PRAYER

Father, my dependence is on You and You alone. Apart from You I can do nothing, but in Christ who strengthens me I can do all things.

DECREE

I decree the enemy tempting me is under my God-surrendered feet. I declare my humility exalts me and qualifies me to walk in great authority, in Jesus's name.

AUGUST

Assuredly, I say to you, whatever you bind on earth will be bound in heaven, and whatever you loose on earth will be loosed in heaven. Again I say to you that if two of you agree on earth concerning anything that they ask, it will be done for them by My Father in heaven. For where two or three are gathered together in My name, I am there in the midst of them.

August 1

Combat the Enemy's Identity Attacks

The enemy has launched verbal attacks against you, up and down and round and about. He wants you to feel as if you're less than. He wants you to feel as if you're not capable of battling him. He wants you to feel as if there is something wrong with you. He wants you to feel shame to the core. But the there is nothing wrong with you. Don't buy into the enemy's identity attacks. You are in Me and I am in you. Stand against the verbal attacks. Let My voice be the loudest you hear.

COLOSSIANS 1:22; 1 THESSALONIANS 1:4; 1 PETER 2:9–10

PRAYER

Father, help me renew my mind to who I really am thanks to Your plan of salvation. Deliver me from identity issues and help me walk worthy of my calling, in Jesus's name.

DECREE

I decree every enemy attack on my identity rebounds off me and confronts the wicked one. I declare I am loved, accepted, capable, and forgiven, in Jesus's name.

My Conviction Is Not Condemnation

Can you discern the difference between My conviction and the enemy's accusatory condemnation? I am the One Who convicts. The devil is the condemner. Our natures are completely opposite. The enemy's condemnation brings a damnable judgment against you. My conviction aims to convince you that you've missed the mark so you can acknowledge the truth, repent, and walk free in Christ. I am the One Who convicts. I am love. The enemy is the condemner. He is the father of lies. Ask Me for a revelation of My love, and you will begin to separate the voices of conviction and condemnation.

JOHN 16:8; 1 JOHN 1:9; 2 CORINTHIANS 7:9–10

PRAYER

Father, help me receive more and more of Your love and help me shut out the voice of condemnation that tries to drive me to run from Your presence when I miss the mark.

DECREE

I decree there is therefore now no condemnation to those who are in Christ Jesus—and I am in Christ Jesus. I declare the weapon of condemnation will not prosper against me, in Jesus's name.

Don't Think It Strange

*D*on't think it strange when a fiery trial comes upon you, as if some strange thing has happened to you. I am not the One bringing the trial. Your adversary, the enemy, wants to try you by fire so hot that you run from My presence and into the temporary comfort of sin. Run to Me instead of running into old behaviors that bring a release to your soul. I will walk with you through the fire. You will emerge refined like gold. I will take what the enemy means for harm in your life and work it for your good. Trust Me.

1 PETER 4:12–13; JAMES 1:2–4; 1 CORINTHIANS 10:13

PRAYER

Father, empower my legs to run to You as fast as I can when the enemy's fiery trial threatens to overtake me. Help me not to resist Your refining fire.

DECREE

I decree fire from hell burns up enemy conspiracies to destroy me. I declare the fire of God burns away common ground with the wicked one, in Jesus's name.

Sow and Believe

*D*on't believe the enemy's lies. When you are a giver, you are not in a financial rut; you are in a season of financial growth that hasn't manifested yet. Like when a farmer sows a seed into the ground, it dies. It appears as if the seed is lost. But he waters the seed day and night. He pulls the weeds from around the seedbed. He waits with expectation and then the harvest comes. First the blade, then the ear, then the full harvest. Sow and believe. Don't let the enemy trick you into canceling your harvest with words of doubt.

JAMES 5:7; MARK 4:27; 2 CORINTHIANS 9:6

PRAYER

Father, I believe You are my provider. I believe Your Word is true. Help me withstand the attacks on my mind that fool my heart into speaking evil words over my harvest.

DECREE

I decree devouring demons are expelled from my harvest field. I declare abundance is my portion and my harvest is plentiful, in Jesus's name.

The Warfare Will Make You Stronger

I will not let you down. I will take you through this, and I will take you over this. I will position you on the mountaintop where you can sing My praises. And you will be stronger for the warfare that you found yourself in. You will be stronger for the season of affliction that you're walking through. It will not kill you. Your flesh may be dying, and your soul may be aching, but it will not kill you. It will make you stronger. Lean on Me when the enemy's attacks make you feel weak. I am your strength.

Isaiah 43:2; 2 Corinthians 4:17; Isaiah 12:2

PRAYER

Father, strengthen me, and I will be strengthened. Put a new song in my heart, and I will rejoice in You despite the incessant attacks on my life. You are My deliverer.

DECREE

I decree my strength is increasing with every swing of the sword. I declare greater is He who is in me than he who is in the world, in Jesus's name.

August 6

Abolish the Enemy's Plans

Stop and abolish the worrisome wondering. Stop and abolish the fearful thoughts and the evil foreboding. Stop and abolish these things that try to steal, kill, and destroy your future. For I have given you a holy imagination to imagine yourself walking in My will, to imagine yourself walking in freedom, to imagine yourself walking in perfect health and joy and peace. But the enemy would come with vain imaginations to contradict that seed of the word that I planted in your heart.

PSALM 91:3; EPHESIANS 3:20–21; 1 CORINTHIANS 2:9

PRAYER

Father, help me abolish those things working to abolish Your will for my life. Help me discern the little foxes spoiling my vine and imagine myself according to Your Word.

DECREE

I decree demonic imaginations are erased in the spirit before I ever see them in my mind. I declare I walk in freedom in every area of my life in Jesus's name.

You Will Rebound from Every Attack

Let go of resentment and let go of bitterness that is attacking your soul after this season of prolonged warfare. Let go of these things and choose not to receive these thoughts that muddy your perspective. Put your heart in My capable hands and cast off these damaging emotions. Understand and know I work all things together for good. That which the enemy used to try to destroy you will ultimately bounce off you. You will rebound from this attack like you rebounded after the last attack. Only let go of bitterness and resentment that hold back your rebound.

HEBREWS 12:15; EPHESIANS 4:31–32; ROMANS 8:28

PRAYER

Father, I put my heart in Your hands because You alone can heal the wounds. You alone can strengthen my spirit. You alone can cleanse me from unrighteousness.

DECREE

I decree what the enemy meant for my harm will become his harm. I declare the enemy's attempts to thwart my perspective are thwarted, in Jesus's name.

Wipe Your Eyes

*W*hen you can't see the victory, wipe your eyes. Wipe away the tears. Wipe away the negativity. Wipe away those things that are causing you some measure of spiritual blindness. Sometimes the enemy uses circumstances as blinders so you can't see to the right or to the left. All you see is down a dark tunnel, and it's discouraging your heart. The blinders keep you from believing My best for you. But I am not blind to your woes and to your discouragement. The enemy has not blinded Me. I see you and I hear you. Ask Me to help you wipe away the enemy's assignment against your vision.

PSALM 119:18; MARK 8:25; REVELATION 21:4

PRAYER

Father, help me wipe the tears from my eyes so I can see You clearly. Help me see past the pain of the last season and the shock of the spiritual attack.

DECREE

I decree woe to the enemy of my soul. I declare discouragement is not my portion because I encourage myself in the Lord like David did, in Jesus's name.

August 9

War in My Grace

ake no mistake, the enemy will not back down. The enemy will not lay down his weapons. The enemy will not stop resisting you. But don't be afraid or dismayed. There is grace upon grace upon grace for those who seek My face. You have to keep pressing, but you have to press My way. Don't press in your own strength. Don't push the world's way. You can't sustain the level I want to take you unless you press My way. If you war in My grace, you will not grow weary in the battle. Do this My way.

JAMES 4:7; JOHN 1:16; 1 JOHN 2:6

PRAYER

Father, help me war in the grace of God. Help me receive Your all-sufficient grace to empower me to win the battle that threatens me at every turn.

DECREE

I decree the thorn in my flesh returns to the enemy and pricks him at every turn. I declare God's grace combats the demonic weariness coming at me, in Jesus's name.

When Sickness Threatens Your Household

*W*hen sickness threatens your household, resist it like you would resist a thief trying to break into your house because that's what it is. Sickness and diseases are tag-team thieves. The spirit of infirmity comes to steal your divine health, to wear down your body, and destroy opportunities to prosper. Resist symptoms of sickness and disease. Resist the temptation to voice your discomfort. Sickness does not come from My Kingdom. Reject it.

PSALM 103:3; PROVERBS 16:24; ISAIAH 53:5

PRAYER

Father, I thank You that by Christ's stripes I am healed. Help me embrace the reality of divine health that Jesus died to give me.

DECREE

I decree the spirit of infirmity is impotent in my life. I declare I was healed at Calvary's cross; I am healed and I walk in divine health, in Jesus's name.

Reject Rejection

Rejection is an insidious enemy that works to destroy your relationships. Refuse to believe the lies of this spirit. Silence the voice of this demon that tempts you to reject others before they can reject you. Yes, people will reject you, but I will never leave you or forsake you. Speak out of your mouth what I say about you. You are accepted and acceptable in Christ. Embrace My love and send rejection packing.

EPHESIANS 1:6; ROMANS 15:7; 1 JOHN 4:8

PRAYER

Father, help me shut down and turn away the voice of rejection in my life, whether it's loud and boisterous or subtle and cunning. Help me embrace Your love.

DECREE

I decree the spirit of rejection is forbidden from access to my soul. I declare I am accepted in the beloved, all day and in every way, in Jesus's name.

Spoil the Spoilers

$\mathcal{D}$etermine to spoil the spoilers. Those demon powers that sneak into your camp and try to rob you of your peace, your joy, and My promises over your life cannot spoil you if you stay alert and vigilant. Watch and pray and you will be less vulnerable to the spoilers that aim to take what belongs to you. Spoil the strategy of the spoilers by staying in the offense. Spoil the spoilers' sinister plots by establishing a hedge of protection. In prayer. Spoil the spoilers.

PROVERBS 22:23; EXODUS 3:22; PSALM 119:62

PRAYER

Father, give me a newfound determination to watch and pray so that the spoilers cannot find their way into my mind, my household, my finances, or my family.

DECREE

I decree the spoilers are spoiled, sabotaged, and separated from my life. I declare I am spoiling the spoilers who spoiled me in past seasons, in Jesus's name.

Choose to Walk Free

I want you to walk free, unencumbered by the strife of the past, by the disappointments of the past, by the ties that bind you to your past. It is time to look ahead with fresh eyes, to move with fresh energy and with a fresh anointing that comes from being willing to let go, to turn the key of finishing, and walk through the new doors I have for you. There are issues in that need to be resolved so you can run the race I have set before you without the heavy weights and toxic trouble of the past. Choose this day to resolve, reconcile, and repent of the old ways so you can move into the new thing I have prepared for you.

PSALM 119:45; ISAIAH 61:1; 2 CORINTHIANS 3:17

PRAYER

Father, help me walk past the ties that bind. Help me walk away from the disappointments and discouragements. Help me walk into the new thing.

DECREE

I decree the doors God has ordained for me are opening up before me. I declare demonic portals over my life are shut down and shut up, in Jesus's name.

Don't Blame Me for Your Warfare

I am not the one that brought the trial. I'm not the one that brought the calamity and the distress. I'm not the one who is warring against you and making you weary. Don't blame Me for your warfare. I've given you authority over the enemy. You overcome him by the blood of the Lamb, the word of your testimony, and your refusal to focus on yourself. Stop focusing on you, you, you. Stop focusing on the devil, the devil, the devil. Start focusing on Me. I am the One who will bring you through the trial, the calamity, the distress, and the warfare. I am for you, not against you.

JAMES 1:2; PSALM 95:8; 1 PETER 4:12

PRAYER

Father, help me never to fall for the temptation to question Your justice and Your mercy. Teach me to keep myself stirred up in my most holy faith.

DECREE

I decree the accuser of the brethren is cast out of my midst. I declare the accusations of the evil one against me, God, or others do not land in my mind or in my heart, in Jesus's name.

August 15

I Am Going to Shake You Loose from Oppression

The enemy has come to oppress you, but I've come to set you free. Before too long, you're going to shake loose of some things that have tried to shake you to pieces. So, don't mind the shaking. Don't let it dismay you. Don't let it bring discouragement to your heart. Just realize I am in it. I am working in it. I am not shaking you up, but I am shaking you free. And you're going to walk in to this next season with a new freedom, with a new liberty, with a new perspective.

EXODUS 3:7–8; JOB 36:15; PSALM 119:134

PRAYER

Father, let me not be disappointed and put to shame. Let me not be shaken off Your promises by the enemy's unjust attacks. Put me back together again.

DECREE

I decree the enemy that seeks to take my life is taken to gross darkness and burned with fire from hell. I declare I am shaking the enemy loose, in Jesus's name.

I Am Shifting You Out of Confusion

The enemy has sown seeds of confusion in your mind so that you no longer see what I see. You see what he wants you to see. He's shaken your confidence in yourself and even your confidence in Me. Know this: I will send confusion into in the enemy's camp as you praise Me. For I will shift you out of that place of confusion and into a place of knowing. I am shifting you out a place of bewilderment and into a place of confidence that you hear My voice. I am shifting you from a place of searching for answers into a place of understanding what My will is. I will do this as you praise Me.

MATTHEW 13:24–25; 1 SAMUEL 14:20; PSALM 103

PRAYER

Father, shift me out of confusion and into confidence in Your name and Your weapons of warfare. Help me break out of bewilderment and into Your wonder.

DECREE

I decree the seeds of confusion the enemy has sown will bring forth a wicked harvest in his own field. I declare I am confident and bold in Christ, in Jesus's name.

Are You Believing a Lie?

*I*f you were deceived would you know it? Of course, you would not know you were deceived because that is the very essence of deception. Do not be afraid, but do not presume you are not believing a lie. If you do not have peace, if you do not have joy, if you do not see breakthrough, if you are not walking in the fullness of your calling, you are believing some sort of lie. You may have learned this as a child or as an adult. It doesn't matter when the deception came. What matters is you break that deception and embrace the truth that keeps you free. Acknowledge the possibility of deception in your life and ask me to break it off your mind.

JAMES 1:22; GALATIANS 6:7; 1 TIMOTHY 4:1

PRAYER

Father, break any and all deception off my mind and my heart. Help me discern the areas of my life where Your Word is not ruling and reigning in my soul.

DECREE

I decree seeds of the devil's dastardly deception are destroyed. I declare that deception cannot stand in my life because I am a lover of the truth, in Jesus's name.

August 18

Enter Into a New Season of Prayer Answers

*Y*ou will enter into a season of prayer answers when you enter a season of prayer. You will see My perfect will come into your circumstances when you pray in faith, nothing wavering. You will see My kingdom come into your life in its fullness when you start persistently asking. So, ask and keep on asking. Then ask again. Stop listening to the voice of doubt. Stop listening to the voice of unbelief. Stop listening to the voice of fear. Stop listening to the voice of unbelieving believers. Listen for My voice. Listen to My voice. Listen to Me. I am inviting you to ask.

JOHN 14:14; MATTHEW 18:19; MARK 11:24

PRAYER

Father, help me remember to turn to You first at all times and with everything. Help me keep on asking and to banish other voices from my soul.

DECREE

I decree the angel wrestling principalities over my prayer answers is winning the fight. I declare when I ask of the Lord, I receive so my joy may be made full, in Jesus's name.

Remember This When You Sleep

The enemy comes while you're asleep to sow vain imaginations, to sow lies and deception, to sow that which is not right and that which is not true. Continue to sow My Word in your heart and My Word will choke out the seeds of the enemy. The enemy's plans and the enemy's weeds are trying to choke out My Word. But as you continue to meditate on Me and who I am and what I've said to you in your secret place—and what I've recorded by My Holy Spirit in Scripture—My Word will choke out the enemy's seed and your life will blossom.

MARK 1:4–20; ROMANS 13:11; PSALM 18:30

PRAYER

Father, help me use Your Word—meditation on Your Word—to build up my faith and to break the enemy's chokehold in my life. Help me cast down vain imaginations.

DECREE

I decree every seed the enemy has sown in my heart has a crop failure. I declare the Word of God sown into my heart will bring forth a harvest of victory, in Jesus's name.

My Love for You Will Overcome

My love for you is perfect, and it grieves my heart to watch the enemy toy with you. My love for you will overcome every tie, stronghold, bondage, and bad habit when you receive the revelation of its strength to cast out everything that gets in its way. I am love. I am your deliverer. I will make a way for you when it doesn't look like there is any possible way. Let the revelation of My love for you strengthen you and deliver you from the enemy's trap of lies.

JOHN 15:13; 1 JOHN 4:16; JOHN 13:34

PRAYER

Father, help me receive You as love so I can receive everything Your love offers—strength, peace, joy, deliverance, healing, and all Your benefits.

DECREE

I decree those who have dug a pit for me will fall into it headlong. I declare all the benefits of God's love are manifesting in my life for His glory, in Jesus's name.

Get Mad with the Devil

*D*on't get mad at Me when things don't go your way. Don't blame Me when you feel like victory is lost. Don't accuse Me because you feel like I didn't help you, didn't protect you, or didn't come through for you. Get mad with the devil. He is the source of your problems. Don't get mad at your friends, mad at your pastor, or mad at your spouse because they didn't give you what you felt you needed when you were in the raging war. Get mad at the devil. Don't get mad at yourself. Get mad at the devil. And use that righteous anger to take him down.

PSALM 7:11; ECCLESIASTES 7:4; JAMES 1:20

PRAYER

Father, help me to place the blame for the killing, stealing, and destruction in my life squarely where it belongs: on the enemy of my soul. Remind me of this truth.

DECREE

I decree the root of my problems is plucked out of my life and destroyed. I declare my righteous indignation fuels me to swing the sword until every foe falls, in Jesus's name.

Don't Let the Devil Dupe You

Don't let the devil dupe you. You are created in My image and my likeness. He wants you to think you are less than. But the greater One lives in you. The Spirit of Christ lives on the inside of you. You are a temple for My Spirit. You are not condemned. There is no condemnation for those who are seated in heavenly places with My Son. There is forgiveness of sins to those who repent. So when the enemy tempts you and you fall, get back up again and run to Me, the greater One. I will strengthen you.

2 CORINTHIANS 11:3; ROMANS 8:1; EPHESIANS 2:6

PRAYER

Father, open my eyes and help me see who I really am in Christ so the enemy can't deceive me with emotions contrary to Your Word. Thank You for the gift of repentance.

DECREE

I decree the enemy's slick lies do not land in my soul. I declare I am forgiven of all my sins and cleansed from all unrighteousness as I confess my sins to my heavenly Father, in Jesus's name.

August 23

Be Willing to Fight

Some people won't fight against cancer. They just lay down and die. Some people won't fight against poverty. They just stay in bondage. Some people won't fight against fear. They just run and hide. You can't get the spoils of war if you don't fight, but when you fight My way you always get the spoils of war. Be willing to fight. Be willing to war. Be willing to go to battle when others won't and for others who can't. I am with you in the battle. It will be worth the fight.

PSALM 51:12; PSALM 57:7; PSALM 119:154

PRAYER

Father, help me see the worth in every fight that comes my way. Help me fight the devil behind the circumstances and force a shift in Jesus's name.

DECREE

I decree the spoils go to the victor and I am the victor in this epic battle because I stand on God's side. I declare I am willing, able, and ready to fight my battles, in Jesus's name.

Ask Me for Wisdom

When you've done all you can do and you've been standing and withstanding, but feel like you can't stand much longer, what do you do? When you've resisted the devil and submitted yourself to God, but the enemy is just not fleeing, what do you do? When you have repented for any open doors, confessed the Word, decreed, declared, pushed back darkness, exercised the binding and loosing keys of the kingdom, commanded the enemy to cease and desist operations, praised your way through and you are still not breaking through, what do you do? Ask Me for wisdom.

JAMES 1:5; JAMES 3:17; LUKE 21:15

PRAYER

Father, pour out Your wisdom liberally upon my heart. Help me see through Your wise eyes so the enemy does not have an upper hand on me.

DECREE

I decree the enemy's wisdom working to penetrate my life is stymied. I declare wisdom from above is pouring over my heart, so I know which weapon to deploy, in Jesus's name.

Regroup, Regather, and Recover All

I know the battle has been lengthy, but you will win. Now regroup and regather to recover all. Surround yourself with people who can help you to push again—people who can help you to make that final rally all the way across the finish line. Surround yourself with those who will lift up your arms like Aaron and Hur lifted up Moses's arms. Stop surrounding yourself with people who don't believe and drag you down into faithlessness. Don't surround yourself with people who are cursing your victory. Surround yourself with those who know how to fight and are willing to fight for you and with you.

1 Samuel 30:8; Exodus 17:12–14; Judges 7:17–22

PRAYER

Father, show me who to walk with and show me who to run with just as You did Gideon and David. Help me align myself with true warriors who seek Your will alone.

DECREE

I decree the illegal seizures of my property cannot stand in the courts of Heaven. I declare angels surround me as I regroup and recoup what is mine, in Jesus's name.

The Enemy Always Overplays His Hand

The enemy always overplays his hand. You can count on it. The enemy is so full of pride and bravado that he will push a little too far and reveal he is the one behind the scenes wreaking havoc on your life. You may think you're just having a bad day or a bad streak until the enemy pushes a little too far and a little too fast with his agenda, and you see it for what it is. The good news is you don't have to wait for him to overplay his hand. Ask Me for discernment now so you can resist him at the onset.

1 CORINTHIANS 12:10; REVELATION 12:10; JAMES 4:7

PRAYER

Father, give me more discernment. Give me the gift of discerning of spirits so that I can see and know what I am dealing with and go on the offense rather than defense.

DECREE

I decree the smoke with which the enemy is trying to cloud my view burns his eyes so he cannot see my next move. I declare I see and overcome, in Jesus's name.

Break Prophetic Words That Are Not True

*Y*es, you need to break word curses, but you also need to break the spirit on a prophetic word over your life that's not accurate. Beloved, the erroneous prophetic word you don't judge is the prophetic word that could send you down the wrong path. Don't believe every prophecy you hear. Test the spirits to see if the Holy Spirit is the One speaking the words you hear. If you accept a prophetic word over your life that didn't come from My Spirit, it could be coming from a demonic power seeking to destroy you. Break the false words.

1 THESSALONIANS 5:21; 1 JOHN 4:1; JAMES 1:5

PRAYER

Father, help me judge rightly the prophetic words spoken over my life. Help me test the spirits and hold fast to that which is good. Help me to embrace the truth.

DECREE

I decree false prophetic words over my life are aborted and their purpose destroyed. I declare the true prophecies over my life are coming to pass, in Jesus's name.

August 28

Resist the Strongman

When the enemy comes at you one way, he will be forced to flee
seven ways—when you resist him. If you don't resist the strongman,
he will come in and take everything that belongs to you. But if you
bind the strongman, you can take back what he stole in the past
season. Your resistance looks like prayer. Your resistance looks like
binding and loosing. Your resistance looks like speaking words of life.
Your resistance looks like obedience. Your resistance looks like faith-
inspired actions. Rise up and resist and you'll recover all.

JAMES 4:7; MATTHEW 12:29; JOHN 14:15

PRAYER

*Father, when the enemy comes at me one way help me rise up
and resist the voice, the temptation, the accusations, and the
devices he uses against me.*

DECREE

*I decree the strongman is bound in the chains he tried to bind me
with. I declare the enemy is fleeing, leaving behind what he stole
in past seasons, in Jesus's name.*

No More Demonic Detours

*N*o more demonic detours! You've allowed the enemy's whispers to take you off track long enough. You've listened to the voice of fear that caused you to turn right instead of left. You've listened to the voice of doubt that caused you to turn left instead of right. You've stood paralyzed by unbelief at the critical fork in the road. You've hit dead end after dead end and roadblock after roadblock because you listened to the wrong navigation system. I am your navigator. Follow Me and record the win.

ROMANS 8:15; JAMES 1:6; MARK 9:23–25

PRAYER

Father, help me avoid the demonic detours that cause me to walk around the same old mountains again and again and again. Help me break out of this satanic rut.

DECREE

I decree roadblocks for enemies trying to make inroads to my life. I declare dead ends make way for better beginnings in every area the devil has meddled, in Jesus's name.

Repel the Enemy's Lies

I have created you in My likeness. I have chosen you and called you My own. Stop listening to the enemy's lies about who you are not and believe Me when I tell you who you are and how much I love you. Stop receiving these emotional terrorism acts against your mind. Stop allowing the manipulation to overpower your will to fight. Repel the lies and embrace My truth. Command the enemy to be silenced. Mute the lying spirit. Revoke the curses against you. Walk in truth.

GENESIS 1:27; PSALM 143:12; PSALM 31:18

PRAYER

Father, give me the audacious boldness to command the enemy in Jesus's name. Help me to stop allowing the enemy to sway my life here and there and out of Your will.

DECREE

I decree emotional terrorist attacks land in the enemy's habitations as demon powers turn on each other in God's presence. I declare word curses are revoked, in the name of Jesus.

Steady Your Gaze on Me

*W*hen you steady your gaze on Me, you will know and understand that I am good, and I've always had your back. And in every war you've fought, I have equipped you for success. I have mantled you for victory. I have sent you forth with an assurance that nothing shall by any means harm you. You are allowing the enemy to harm you. It's not Me allowing it. You are allowing the enemy to beat you down. It's not Me allowing it. I have called you to rise up. I have plans to lift you up. Agree with Me and ascend.

PSALM 27:4; ACTS 7:55; LUKE 10:19

PRAYER

Father, help me steady my gaze on You when everything and everyone around me demands my immediate attention. Help me get in full agreement with Your plans for my life.

DECREE

I decree my enemies are taken away in a whirlwind of God's righteous anger. I declare my eyes shall stay fixed on the God of my salvation, in Jesus's name.

SEPTEMBER

Blessed is the man who walks not in the counsel of the ungodly, nor stands in the path of sinners, nor sits in the seat of the scornful; but his delight is in the law of the Lord, and in His law he meditates day and night. He shall be like a tree planted by the rivers of water, that brings forth its fruit in its season, whose leaf also shall not wither; and whatever he does shall prosper.

PSALM 1:1–3

You Can Withstand the Pressure

*W*hen you come out of the season of testing at the devil's hand, you will be stronger. You will be wiser. You will be more ready and able to walk into the blessing I have prepared for you and the calling I have prepared for you before the foundation of the earth. Don't reject the pressure that comes from My Spirit. Resist the pressure that comes from the enemy because it's stalling you and keeping you in this holding pattern. But embrace My pressure because it is molding you and shaping you into the image of My dear Son.

PSALM 118:5–6; 1 PETER 1:6–7; ROMANS 8:29

PRAYER

Father, prepare me for the blessings to chase me down and overtake me. Help me break free from the holding pattern of hell and see Heaven come down in my life.

DECREE

I decree demonic pressure against me is reversed and crushes the enemy's plan for this season of my life. I declare I can do all things through Christ who gives me strength, in Jesus's name.

September 2

Your Sowing Is an Act of War

Let your seed be a weapon and your sowing an act of war. When you give into My Kingdom, when you sow your seed even when you have only a handful left, you are wielding the seed like a weapon against lack. Your sowing becomes an act of war against the fearful imaginations in your mind. Your demonstration of trust in My Word and My promises of provision pushes the enemy off your harvest. When you keep sowing even though you are not seeing the fruit, you can be sure the fruit will be abundant when the crop comes in.

2 CORINTHIANS 9:7; MATTHEW 6:21; PROVERBS 11:24–25

PRAYER

Father, help me overcome the fear of letting go. Instill in my heart confidence to sow and smother the enemy's voice of fear in my life. I wage war with my seed.

DECREE

I decree war on the enemy of my harvest with my generous seed. I declare the seed in my hand will advance the Kingdom of light and damage the kingdom of darkness, in Jesus's name.

Why Not Praise Me Now?

*N*o matter what weapon the enemy has formed against you, I will not allow you to come into permanent harm. You are walking through the warfare, and I am walking through it with you. As you walk with Me, you will see and know that I am praiseworthy. So, why not praise Me now? Why not let your praise be a weapon while you walk through enemy fire? Why wait until you feel like praising Me? Praise Me by faith. In your praise you will find strength and you will find purpose and you will find new life. Your praise demonstrates to the enemy that your trust is in Me—and that trust will see you through to victory.

ISAIAH 54:17; PSALM 150:1–6; ISAIAH 25:1

PRAYER

Father, I praise you by faith in Your Word. I praise You because You are the strength of my life. I praise You because You always lead me into triumph. I praise You.

DECREE

I decree my praises disorient and demoralize the enemy powers seeking my life. I declare God inhabits my praises and shields me from all enemy attack, in Jesus's name.

September 4

When You Feel Like You're Dying Inside

*E*ven though you feel like you're dying on the inside, even though you feel like it's never going to change, even though you feel like you have nowhere else to turn and no matter where you go it's another enemy attack, I am with you. I will pour out My Spirit upon you, and I will refresh you if you'll stop looking at things the way they are and begin to look at things the way I told you they would be. If you will put your faith in Me and put your hope in Me and put your trust in Me, I will deliver you from this place more quickly than you think.

1 CORINTHIANS 3:16; MARK 11:22–24; PSALM 9:10

PRAYER

Father, help me to tap into faith instead of letting my feelings tap out my emotional energy. Teach me how to lean completely on You for everything.

DECREE

I decree death to the enemy's plots and schemes against my destiny. I declare my faith is in the faithful God who delivers me from the cords of death, in Jesus's name.

I Will Put My Words in Your Mouth

*D*o not fret; do not worry because it only leads to evil. Stop thinking about the bad things that could happen. Begin to think about what I've told you can happen, what I've told you is possible, because all things are possible to those who believe. And this mind traffic that comes to steal your joy, you've got to release it. You've got to refuse to accept it. You've got to stop dwelling on things that you could do nothing about and realize I am the God of "all things are possible." I am the God of reconciliation. I am the God of provision and restitution. I am the God who has your back.

HEBREWS 13:6; LUKE 1:37; MATTHEW 19:26

PRAYER

Father, help me overcome the anxiety that plagues my heart when I can't figure out what to do. Help me lean in to Your promises by faith in Your Son.

DECREE

I decree plagues into the enemy's camp that force him to let go of my mind, will, and emotions. I declare God's words will guide and frame my life, in Jesus's name.

September 6

I See You

I see you. I see you in the faith. I see you pressing on toward the mark. I see you blessed and prosperous. I see you healed and whole. I see you delivered, set apart, sanctified, anointed, and appointed. I see you carrying the mantle that I have given you and doing great exploits for Me. I see you in these ways. How do you see yourself? Allow yourself to see yourself the way I see you, and don't allow the enemy to paint a different picture of you. I see you as complete in Christ. I see you. I see you through the trials, and I see you through the tribulations. I see you and I hear you and I am with you.

PROVERBS 15:3; 2 CHRONICLES 16:9; PSALM 33:13

PRAYER

Father, thank You for taking notice of my plight and for Your promises to help me. Give me a greater revelation of who I am in Christ and Your faithfulness toward me.

DECREE

I decree blindness into the evil watchers who look into my life and report back to principalities and powers. I declare God watches over me carefully, in Jesus's name.

September 7

You Are Well Able to Win the Next Battle

*D*on't shrink back now. Don't allow yourself to feel inadequate to fight the battles that await you in the days ahead. I have gone before you to secure the victory. You war from a position of victory in heavenly places. All you have to do is follow Me. I've never promised you a rose garden. I've never promised you a life without trouble. In this world there will be tribulation but rejoice because I have overcome the world. Keep Me in mind and keep My Word in your heart and keep Me at the forefront of your communications. I'll tell you what to do next.

2 CORINTHIANS 10:3–6; JOHN 16:33; ISAIAH 58:11

PRAYER

Father, help me to follow You into each and every day, into each and every battle, and into each and every victory. Help me not to neglect Your preparation and Your presence.

DECREE

I decree tribulation into the enemy's squadrons, who must tremble at God's Word. I declare I am well able to break through enemy opposition, in Jesus's name.

September 8

Be of Good Cheer

I see the mountain standing before you but be of good cheer. I see the wilderness you're walking through. Be of good cheer. I see the cave, the corner the enemy has backed you into. Be of good cheer because My joy is your strength. Choose to tap into My unlimited joy and let it wash over you. Allow Me to strengthen you. Allow My joy to be a safeguard for you. Do not allow yourself to be troubled. I see what you see, and I have a plan for you to move through every enemy obstacle into your promises.

JOHN 16:24; 1 PETER 1:8; ROMANS 14:17

PRAYER

Father, help me maintain joy when the enemy is arranging circumstantial evidence to depress and oppress my soul. Help me see obstacles as opportunities.

DECREE

I decree the enemies that seek my shame are confounded. I declare the joy of the Lord is my strength and oppression does not come near me, in Jesus's name.

Disconnect from Stumbling Blocks

Don't be afraid and don't delay in moving away from those who have become consistent stumbling blocks in your life, those who want to hold you back, those who have jealousy in their heart and envy in their soul toward you because you've going somewhere they cannot go. The enemy will inspire people to conspire against you in their own heart even though they know it's wrong. The enemy will inspire them to tear you down because they want what you have but they're not willing to do what you did to get it. Be kind. Show love. Pray for them but stop giving the enemy access to your life through them.

PROVERBS 13:20; 2 CORINTHIANS 5:16; PROVERBS 14:7

PRAYER

Father, help me disconnect from the people who are unhealthy for my spiritual walk. Help me walk in love but not walk so close that my destiny is at risk of delay.

DECREE

I decree demon powers conspiring against me meet with God's judgment swiftly. I declare I walk in kindness with people, but I am ruthless toward demons, in Jesus's name.

September 10

The Enemy Fire Will Not Burn You

I have not forsaken you in this battle. I know it feels like the warfare is too great, but I have promised not to allow more to come upon you than you can bear. I know the burdens the enemy has placed on your shoulders feels too intense to carry, but I've invited you to cast your cares on Me because I care for you. I know the fiery trial seems overwhelming, but when you walk through enemy fire, it will not burn you because I am your shield and buckler. I have not forsaken you in this battle. Trust Me. I am still with you.

PSALM 37:27–29; PSALM 46:1; ISAIAH 62:4

PRAYER

Father, thank You that You are faithful to stand with me as I withstand by Your grace what is standing against me. If You are for me, I can stand against anything.

DECREE

I decree the enemy is burned with the fire he has planned to burn me with. I declare feeling overwhelmed is underwhelming to my soul because I trust in God, in Jesus's name.

Ask for My Will

*A*sking for My will is an assault on the enemy's kingdom because it unlocks My plans for your life in the earth. Ask and receive that your joy may be made full. Pray bold prayers. Pray accurate prayers. Pray with the end in mind. See My will in your heart and pray My will through your mouth, then do it again and again and again. Ask and keep on asking. You can ask Me anything. I am listening to your heart's cries. I am working all things together for good. Keep making the ask. Let's start praying.

1 THESSALONIANS 5:17; MATTHEW 6:19–20; 1 PETER 4:19

PRAYER

Father, help me pray with the end in mind. Help me see Your will for my life and give me the tenacity to ask and keep on asking even when I don't see things changing.

DECREE

I decree the enemy of God's will for my life is ashamed and confused by his own audacity. I declare God hears me and answers me when I call, in Jesus's name.

September 12

Decide Enough Is Enough

If you'll just stare at Jesus, if you'll just worship Me, if you'll just get in your Bible, if you'll just bind the enemy, if you'll just loose the angels, if you'll just repent of backing up and allowing the enemy to take your ground, if you'll just take authority over the wicked one, if you'll just come against him in Christ's name, if you'll just plead the blood, if you'll just cast down vain imaginations, if you'll just stand and keep on standing, I won't do your part, but I'll help you do your part. My grace is sufficient for this battle. Just decide enough is enough, claim your victory, and exercise your faith.

ROMANS 16:20; REVELATION 12:11; MATTHEW 18:18

PRAYER

Father, help me do all of what the Word teaches. Put in me a righteous indignation against the enemies of Your Kingdom so I will not tolerate the wicked workings of hell against me.

DECREE

I decree the blood of Jesus drives away every enemy that tries to cross me. I declare the enemy's plans that were once tolerated are now castrated, in Jesus's name.

I Will Redeem Your Forfeiture

*Y*ou have learned and you have grown in grace since that day that you forfeited the fight and threw in the towel. You have gained wisdom and revelation since that day you couldn't stay in the fight. Now it's time to confront the enemies you were too timid to confront in the past. This is your season to run toward the fight. I will strengthen your hamstrings. I will strengthen your calf muscles. I will make your feet like hinds' feet so you will not slip, and you will not fall. You will sprint, and you will make up for lost time because you've determined in your heart to do My will. You've learned the lessons of the past season. Rise up now and run by faith toward the fight from which you once ran. You win!

PROVERBS 24:16; PSALM 37:4; ROMANS 5:3–5

PRAYER

Father, thank You for giving me second, third, fourth, and fifth chances when I forfeit the fight. Help me learn the lessons from the last battle so I break into victory.

DECREE

I decree the intimidating power of God forces the enemy to forfeit this fight. I declare my feet are like hinds' feet and I am ascending to God's holy hill, in Jesus's name.

September 14

There Is Strength in Numbers

Try a new way. Try a new thing. The familiar ways of warfare didn't bring swift victory because it wasn't the right strategy. The familiar strategy didn't take you over the top of the mountain opposing you because it wasn't My way for this battle. Seek My strategy. Seek the divine battle connections. Seek those I've called to fight with and for you. Seek those who I've called you to run with. Run to your company of spiritual warriors and put your collective enemies to flight. Stand together and you will push back tens of thousands of demons coming against you.

MATTHEW 18:20; ECCLESIASTES 4:9; ACTS 4:23–24

PRAYER

Father, show me the new way and I'll try it. Teach me the new way and I'll walk it. Help me not get in a spiritual warfare rut but to see the new strategy You've set before me.

DECREE

I decree my battle strategy puts a stranglehold on satan's minions. I declare the might of God working in me pushes back demon powers coming at me, in Jesus's name.

September 15

The Demonic Wall Will Fall

*D*emon powers cannot wall you out of My blessings because you have authority over every demonic wall. Speak to the walls and command them to crumble. Shout at the walls and command them to come down. Sing as you walk around the walls, around the perimeter, around the inside, and around the outside. Sing and praise and watch My power fall, then watch the demonic walls fall. That wall—that fortress that has caused you to feel isolated, to feel obscure, to feel overwhelmed, to feel hopeless—will come down!

JOSHUA 6; 1 JOHN 3:8; EPHESIANS 6:10

PRAYER

Father, help me pray prayers that cause Your power to fall so the wall will fall. Teach me to sing and shout down the boundaries and barriers the enemy has erected.

DECREE

I decree the walls that bound me in are crumbling before my eyes. I declare isolation, obscurity, overwhelmed emotions, and hopelessness are broken off my life, in Jesus's name.

I Am Your Peace in the War

I am your peace in the midst of the war. I am the hope of your life in the midst of the battle. I am the lifter of your head when you are discouraged by the enemy's plots and plans against you. I am calling you to look upward now—to look to My throne of grace. I am the source of your overcoming. I am the demon-conquering power that is in you. I am He who gives you grace sufficient to overwhelm the enemy. I am your victory. Now stand up, look up, and rise up. It's time to swing the sword again.

NUMBERS 6:24–26; PSALM 139:17-18; ROMANS 8:6

PRAYER

Father, I will look to You as my hope and my peace, the lifter of my head and the lover of my soul. Make me stand. Strengthen me to swing Your sword.

DECREE

I decree my bold prayers cause the enemy to misfire his fiery darts. I declare I look up, from where my redemption draws nigh and my victory lies, in Jesus's name.

When People Put Their Mouths All Over You

Those who have wronged you and those who have spit in your face and those who have put their mouths all over you again and again and again are under the influence of the evil one. There is a day of reckoning. Judgement day will come. They will have to give an account for every evil word they said and every evil action they took against you if they do not repent. So, pray for them without ceasing. Pray for them as you would pray for the one you love most in the world, even though you don't like them at all. Pray for those who despitefully use you.

LUKE 22:3; LUKE 6:28; MATTHEW 12:35

PRAYER

Father, help me keep my mouth in line with Your Word. Help me keep my prayers in line with Your will, then I know you will hear my cries and deliver me from evil decrees.

DECREE

I decree a day of reckoning over demon powers that reckoned me defeated. I declare every evil action the enemy took against me will ricochet back at him, in Jesus's name.

When the Enemy Comes in Like a Flood

There are times when the enemy will come in like a flood. But it doesn't always start out like a flood. The enemy is looking for cracks in your foundation. His little lies that may seem insignificant on the surface will seep through those cracks if you let them. But no lie is insignificant. If he can find a crack in your foundation or make a crack in your faith, he can trickle in imaginations that torment your mind. If he can widen the gap, he can come in like a flood. When the enemy comes in like a flood, I will raise a standard against him. But you have to align yourself with that standard. Stand on the Word and the flood will not overtake you.

ISAIAH 59:19; PSALM 50:15; PSALM 46:10

PRAYER

Father, help me experience Your flood of peace in the battle. Teach me to walk in your river of joy in the warfare. Help me flood the Heavens with accurate prayers.

DECREE

I decree the flood of oppression will overtake demon powers rising up against me. I declare I walk according to the standards of God's truth, in Jesus's name.

September 19

When Leviathan Rears His Ugly Head

$\mathcal{L}$eviathan is a twisting serpent. It's a hard-hearted spirit. It's ugly and haughty and full of pride. When someone under Leviathan's influence attacks you, they will put words in your mouth, find offense with you, and flee—or they will attack you with false accusations and break covenant with you. People operating under a Leviathan spirit can't be reasoned with. Go low. Walk in humility. Move in the opposite spirit. Don't engage in the verbal quarrel. Praise Me. I will protect you.

ISAIAH 27:1; PSALM 74:14; PROVERBS 11:2

PRAYER

Father, help me discern the workings of Leviathan and its witchcraft. Help me walk with an unoffendable and humble heart so this spirit can find no place in me.

DECREE

I decree every twisting serpent is tied up in knots. I declare Leviathan's witchcraft does not move me from the place of humility and truth, in Jesus's name.

Diffuse the Ticking Time Bomb

The enemy's lies are like a ticking time bomb. If you don't diffuse the wicked one's destructive lies, they will blow up in your face at the worst possible time. If you don't dismantle the web of lies, they will entrap you in your own soul. Don't put up with a single lie of the enemy. Cast it down. Speak the truth. Don't believe about yourself anything that I have not said in My Word or whispered to your heart. Don't believe about others anything but the best without absolute proof. Don't believe ill of Me. I am on your side. The devil is a liar. He'll try anything.

2 PETER 2:1; JEREMIAH 17:9; PSALM 10:7

PRAYER

Father, help me hear the enemy's ticking time bomb without fear. Give me the right words to combat the enemy's lies and reject the accuser of the brethren.

DECREE

I decree the enemy's time bomb is diffused and ineffective against my life. I declare I shall speak the truth in love and the sword in my mouth cuts through enemy lies, in Jesus's name.

Walk in Peace in a Time of War

There's a time for peace and a time for war. What you need to learn is how to walk in peace in a time of war. These two concepts are not foreign to one another. Yes, there are times of peace and seasons of rest. But you can have peace despite the enemy's best-laid plans. You can rest in the battle as you trust in Me. You can choose to hold your peace when the enemy is working overtime to tempt your tongue. You can do all things through Christ who gives you strength. Ask Me to help you walk in peace even as you walk through the battlefield. I am your peace.

ECCLESIASTES 3:8; ISAIAH 26:3–4; HEBREWS 4:3

PRAYER

Father, You have created me for war. Help me walk in peace when demon powers are working to kill, steal, and destroy the inheritance Christ willed to me in His new covenant.

DECREE

I decree the enemy of my peace is plagued with discord, disharmony, and distress. I declare I walk in the supernatural peace of God, in Jesus's name.

September 22

Embrace the Mind of Christ

The enemy works to cloud your mind with witchcraft and skew your sensibilities. The enemy works to show you a cracked image of yourself in his warped mirror. Set your mind, and keep it set on things above. Keep your mind on Me rather than on yourself. Know and understand that you are always on My mind. My thoughts toward you are greater than the number of sand grains on the seashore. Not only is My mind on you, I have victory in mind for you. Embrace the mind of Christ especially when the enemy wants to cloud your mind and show you wrong pictures of yourself.

PHILIPPIANS 2:5–8; 1 CORINTHIANS 2:6; PSALM 139:17-18

PRAYER

Father, thank You for Your timely instruction and for always keeping me aware of the enemy's plots. Help me see myself rightly and remember Your victory.

DECREE

I decree the witchcraft mission the enemy is releasing on my mind miscarries. I declare my mind is steadily meditating on the Word of God and I think clearly, in Jesus's name.

Speak the Name Above All Names

When the enemy seeks to put you in bondage of any kind, speak the name of Jesus with a confidence that His name carries supernatural power that supersedes the enemy's dark power. Before the enemy can ensnare you in his trap, speak the name of Jesus that breaks the chains the enemy plans to wrap around you. Speak the name of Jesus that causes enemies to flee before you, behind you, and from round and about you. Trust in Me and you will not suffer shame. Speak the name that is above all names, and watch the chains break and fall to the ground as the enemy bows in shame.

PHILIPPIANS 2:9; ACTS 4:12; JOHN 14:3

PRAYER

Father, help me keep the name above all names in my mouth. Show me plainly how powerful that name is as I choose to speak that name instead of complain.

DECREE

I decree every enemy that comes against me shall bow in shame to the name above all names. I declare the name above all names shall continually be in my mouth, in Jesus's name.

Know Your Weaknesses

The only perfect warrior to walk the earth was Jesus Himself. As for you, know your weaknesses. Understand the ways in which the enemy has been successful in the past of tempting you away from My heart or finding an open door in your soul. The enemy has been studying humankind for thousands of years, and demon watchers keep an eye on you. The wicked one knows your weaknesses, so you need to know them also. Armed with this knowledge, you can cooperate with Me to strengthen yourself in those areas and shut the enemy out of your heart and mind.

2 CORINTHIANS 12:9–11; ZECHARIAH 4:6; EPHESIANS 6:10

PRAYER

Father, show me by Your gentle Spirit the weaknesses in my soul You are ready to deal with, and I will yield to You. Make me more sensitive to Your Spirit.

DECREE

I decree the enemy's gruesome grip over my soul is weakening as I face the truth that sets me free. I declare where I am weak my God in Heaven is strong, in Jesus's name.

When the Enemy Uses People Close to You

The devil knows how to hit you where it hurts, but he needs to get close enough to launch a fiery dart that hits your heart. The enemy uses people to hurt you, to wound you, to judge you, to frustrate you, to argue with you, and the like. You know that. Unfortunately, the enemy will take any chance he can to use the people closest to you because they have the ultimate access. When the enemy uses people close to you against you, forgive them. Speaking the truth in love, tell them how the enemy worked against you and work together to prevent a repeat attack.

PSALM 59:1–2; PSALM 52:8–9; PSALM 56:9

PRAYER

Father, help me walk in love when the enemy uses people close to me to hurt me, wound me, judge me, frustrate me, and argue with me without a cause.

DECREE

I decree my spiritual foes are plucked out of hiding and cast into darkness. I declare I walk in forgiveness toward people the enemy uses, in Jesus's name.

You Are the Retaliation

Retaliation is real. The enemy of your soul will strike back after a great victory, just like Jezebel struck back at Elijah after the showdown at Mount Carmel. The enemy of your soul will wait for the most opportune time to creep in and take his best shot in the name of retaliation. As for you, don't fear retaliation with your every move. Don't dread the retaliation as if you will fall at the hand of the enemy. Expect it. Brace for it. Go on the offensive. Say within your heart, "I am the retaliation." I am backing you up. Bind the retaliation.

LUKE 4:13; EPHESIANS 4:27; MATTHEW 18:18

PRAYER

Father, help me shift my mind-set from a defensive only posture to an offensive posture. Help me see that I am the retaliation against the enemies that viciously attack Your will.

DECREE

I decree every retaliatory devil power rising up against me is burned up under holy fire. I declare I am the retaliation and the enemy has no upper hand on me in Christ, in Jesus's name.

Thwart Emotional Assaults

Do not be afraid of the terror by night or the arrow that flies by day, but rather lift up your shield of faith and quench these fiery darts. Block the word curses and evil decrees launched against you to set your life on hell. Thwart these emotional assaults against your mind and against your life. I will give you strength and grace, but you must gird up the loins of your mind. I can't do that for you. You must choose to reject what the enemy tells you about yourself. Your identity is in Christ. You are a new creature. Old things have passed away.

1 PETER 1:13; PSALM 91; 2 CORINTHIANS 5:17

PRAYER

Father, I will not fear, and I will not be dismayed. Protect me from the terror, the arrows, the word curses, the evil decrees, and the emotional assaults and give me peace.

DECREE

I decree the net the fowler hid for my feet snares him swiftly. I declare my identity is in Christ, I carry His authority, and I walk in His victory, in Jesus's name.

Reject the Enemy's Bait

I want to do a new thing in your life, but you have to let Me. You have to allow Me entrance into your heart and into your mind and let My thoughts and My strategies flood your soul. When you begin listening to the devil, you get stuck. Don't chew on the enemy's bitter bait. If you'll just chew on My Word—if you'll just get caught up in My Spirit—you will see that the new beginning you've been crying out for will no longer elude you. The moment you say yes to My heart and shut out the enemy, your new beginning has started. Your new beginning will manifest in that moment. All you have to do then is step into it.

LAMENTATIONS 3:22–23; ISAIAH 43:18–19; ROMANS 6:4

PRAYER

Father, help me let go of the old thoughts, the old memories, the old habits and patterns, and help me embrace the new work You want to do in my mind, my spirit, and my life.

DECREE

I decree old enemies are fainting in the face of my authority. I declare I am entering into the new things God has prepared for me in this season, in Jesus's name.

September 29

Learn to Say No

𝒴ou are the only one in your life who can make the decision to say, "No, I will not think on these things the enemy is speaking to my mind." Philippians 4 tells you plainly to think on things that are good and pure and lovely and of a good report and honorable. When you choose to make that shift in your mind, you will see that there is a shift in your heart. Then you will notice there's a shift in your life, and then you will see a shift in your family. Then you will see a shift in your finances. But it all starts in your own mind and in your own mouth.

Matthew 5:37; Colossians 3:23; Proverbs 3:5

PRAYER

Father, You know how to say no. Will you teach me? Will you give me the courage? Will you help me overcome the fear of man? Will you help me wait on You?

DECREE

I decree destruction upon my enemy of my destiny, that it comes against him unawares. I declare no man on earth or devil in hell can manipulate God's will for my life, in Jesus's name.

Sing My Tune

*G*et in agreement with Me and sing My tune, because I am the One who is singing over you, smiling over you, and watching over you. The enemy is singing a different tune—a tune that is harmful, fearful, and full of death and destruction, because he seeks to steal, kill, and destroy your life. But know this, I can interrupt the demonic recordings playing like a broken record in your soul. I can cut the tape, but I need your help. I need you to tune your ear into My frequency. I need you to put your eyes on My Word so I can do My part and you can do your part and together we can dance again.

1 CORINTHIANS 14:15; HEBREWS 13:15; ZEPHANIAH 3:17

PRAYER

Father, help me get in tune with the songs You are singing over me. Help me tune out the devil's diabolical rapping against my soul. I want to sing a new song.

DECREE

I decree the enemy's arrows flying toward me are broken to pieces. I declare demonic recordings playing in my mind yield to the song of victory in Christ, in Jesus's name.

OCTOBER

Have no fellowship with the unfruitful works of darkness, but rather expose them. For it is shameful even to speak of those things which are done by them in secret. But all things that are exposed are made manifest by the light, for whatever makes manifest is light.

EPHESIANS 5:11–13

October 1

Jesus Is Praying for You

The enemy will come from time to time to sift you like wheat. The enemy sifted Job, and he saw things in himself he didn't like. The enemy sifted Peter, and he saw things in himself that he never knew were there. The enemy will come at times to sift you, but remember, Jesus is praying for you. The enemy will come to test you and try you, working to find a place in you, hoping to cause you to deny Christ, to depart the faith, to give up on the hope of glory. Hold on to Me. I am holding on to you. The sifting will purify you and give you strength.

LUKE 22:31; HEBREWS 7:25; JOHN 10:28

PRAYER

Father, strengthen me through the times of sifting so I can withstand the attack of the enemy against my faith. Purify my heart, and I will worship You all the more.

DECREE

I decree my faith shall not be shipwrecked, but it grows stronger as I meditate on God's Word. I declare the sifting will lead to a shifting toward greater victory, in Jesus's name.

Rise Up with Radical Perseverance

Rise up with a radical perseverance. Rise up with a mind-set that says I will not be moved. The devil can't move you unless you let him move you. If you are being moved in your resolve, if you are being moved in your emotions, understand and know that you are allowing the enemy to weaken you by way of thoughts that are demonic in nature. These vain imaginations are coming to plague your soul. They are coming to move you off My will. They are coming to stir up your emotions. Don't allow yourself to be moved.

JAMES 1:12; 1 CHRONICLES 16:11; EPHESIANS 6:18

PRAYER

Father, give me an enduring spirit and a persevering heart. Make me like the widow who continued petitioning the unjust judge until she obtained justice.

DECREE

I decree my perseverance will gain me the prize on which I have my eyes. I declare justice against every enemy power plaguing my soul is my portion, in Jesus's name.

October 3

You Will Rise Above It

*E*ven when you can't see where you're walking, know that I am with you. I promise to lead you and guide you. I am not a man that I should lie nor the son of man that I should repent. If I say a thing, I will do a thing. I will not leave you without help. I will not leave you without comfort. I will not leave you without provision. When have you seen the righteous forsaken or his children begging for bread? Trust Me in this warfare. The turbulence is only temporary. You will rise above it as you wait upon Me to show you the way. You will see a new perspective when you wait upon Me to show you My way.

JOHN 16:13; NUMBERS 23:19; JEREMIAH 17:7–8

PRAYER

Thank You, Lord, that You will never leave me or forsake me. Help me discern Your presence and Your strength even when I can't hear Your voice instructing me.

DECREE

I decree turbulence must cease, and I curse the root of the attack against my rising. I declare even when I can't feel God, I know He's moving on my behalf, in Jesus's name.

Break the Cycle

*I*t's time to break the cycle, and it's time to bust out of that circle. I've not called you to live in a box. I've not called you to walk in a circle. I've not called you to stand still. I've called you to advance. Stop overthinking it. Look to Me and listen to My voice because My voice is the only true one. There are many voices in the spirit world, but Mine is the only one that speaks with love. Mine is the only one that speaks with peace. Mine is the only one that speaks with joy unspeakable and is full of glory. My voice is the only one that you can trust.

JOHN 10:27; ISAIAH 30:21; JOHN 6:63

PRAYER

Father, lead me into Your cycles—cycles of ever-increasing love, holiness, joy, and peace. Help me tune my ear to Your trustworthy voice.

DECREE

I decree every demonic cycle manifesting in my life is broken in the spirit and the natural. I declare I am in God's rhythm and timing, in Jesus's name.

Don't Fret Over Evildoers

*F*ret not yourself because of evildoers, because of those who prosper in their way. Their prosperity that is built with deceptive practices and their prosperity that is built with envious motives and their prosperity that is built with spite and competition in their heart will not last. So, pray for those who try to trip you up, and pray for those who have become stumbling blocks in your life because I, Myself, love them with a passionate love, but I hate what they're doing. You must love the person as I do but hate the sin.

JOHN 14:23; PSALM 37:7–8; 1 PETER 4:8

PRAYER

Father, help me not to get so upset and angry when I see bad people reap good rewards at my expense. Create in me a clean heart that's willing to pray for them.

DECREE

I decree every person with wrong motives against me is found out and expelled. I declare my discernment about evildoers is accurate, in Jesus's name.

Set Your Forehead Like Flint

*P*repare yourself for war. Get ready for the next battle before it rises against you. Press into My strength so you can be strong in Me and the power of My might. Set your forehead like flint and determine to reach your destiny despite the spiritual opposition that will come along your path. My Word is true. Submit yourself to Me. Resist the devil that's resisting you. He will flee. You will accomplish your assignment.

LUKE 14:31; JOEL 3:9; EZEKIEL 3:9

PRAYER

Father, as I prepare myself for war, give me the insight I need from the last war. Give me whatever I am lacking in wisdom to complete the assignment You've given me.

DECREE

I decree the opposition trips and falls over their own feet. I declare my forehead is set like flint, and no devil in hell is going to stop my God-given mission, in Jesus's name.

Vengeance Is Mine

The avenger may come to plague your house, but vengeance is Mine. I will repay. The avenger will come to carry out vengeance from the word curses of your enemies, but vengeance is Mine. I will repay. The avenger is loosed against you as people in their anger begin to malign you, gossip about you, and otherwise release the power of death against you, but vengeance is Mine. I will repay. You forgive and bless your enemies. I will take vengeance on the avenger for your sake.

PSALM 8:2; ROMANS 12:19; DEUTERONOMY 32:35

PRAYER

Father, help me not to take matters into my own hands in the aftermath of an enemy attack. Help me wait upon You for Your vengeance against the wicked ones.

DECREE

I decree every avenger who has set his sights on my destruction is burned with double fire. I declare my salvation, and that of God, in Jesus's name.

October 8

No Weapon Formed Against You Shall Prosper

*D*id you not hear? Do you not understand? No weapon formed against you shall prosper. Yes, the weapons are strategically crafted. Yes, the enemy organizes in formation. Yes, the fiery darts will launch against you. Yes, it may feel like the weapons are succeeding against you. But ultimately no enemy weapon will take you out or take you down as your soul prospers. Meditate on your victory in Christ. Meditate on who you are and what I've promised you. Believe Me.

ISAIAH 54:17; EPHESIANS 6:16; ROMANS 8:37

PRAYER

Father, thank You for reminding me that although the weapons form, they will not take me out. Help me remember that when the darts are flying at me fast and furious.

DECREE

I decree no weapon formed against me shall prosper. I declare that my arms are strong to hold up the shield of faith my mighty God has put into my hands, in Jesus's name.

When Everything Around You—and in You—Is Shaking

*E*ven when it feels like everything around you is shaking, and everything on the inside of you is shaking, rest assured that no devil in hell can shake you free from My hand. Nothing can shake you loose from my love, because I am with you. I am for you, and if I am for you, who can be against you? In a little while, I am going to shake you loose of some things that have tried to shake your faith. I am going to shake you loose of the enemy's oppression. I am working in the shaking, but I am not shaking you up. I am shaking you free. You will walk out of the shaking with new freedom and a new perspective.

HEBREWS 12:7; PSALM 6:2; PSALM 16:8

PRAYER

Father, stabilize my soul when I feel like the enemy is shaking me off the truth of Your Word. Shake me free from the enemy's grip on my mind.

DECREE

I decree the enemy is shaking and trembling at my God-guaranteed victory. I declare nothing shall by any means stop me from walking in my destiny, in Jesus's name.

Refocus on the Fight at Hand

*Y*ou will win this fight, but you have to press harder than you've pressed before. The enemy has tried to get you to give up and quit. The enemy has caused you to shrink back from the fight because you're so close to the brink of supernatural victory and overwhelming success that he is scared. He's tried every little last thing, but if you will just press a little harder, if you will push a little longer, if you will turn off the TV and put down your phone and pick up your sword, you will deal the victory blow swiftly. Refocus yourself. Rise and fight again. The victory is yours.

PROVERBS 24:16; ISAIAH 59:19; 1 CORINTHIANS 16:13

PRAYER

Father, I repent for shrinking back and running from the battle line instead of to the battle line. Help me get my armor back on and run with my sword in hand back to the fight.

DECREE

I decree the enemy's plans are on the brink of disaster at the hand of my sword. I declare I am focused to fight and win, in Jesus's name.

Use My Word Like a Hammer

I have not walled you out of My presence, but the enemy has come to steal, kill, and destroy by making you feel as if you cannot break through. But I, Myself, am your breakthrough. Celebrate Me. Sing to Me. Lift up My name in your life. Begin to look at Me. Your redemption is secure. Your salvation has been paid for. Everything you have need of belongs to you in the spirit. Speak to the wall. Take My Word and use it like a hammer and knock down that wall, brick by brick. There's the strategy to breaking through the enemy resistance.

JEREMIAH 23:29; MARK 11:23; MICAH 2:13

PRAYER

Father, thank You for sending Jesus to be my breakthrough. I will speak Your Word to walls of opposition, stumbling blocks, and every mountain in the way of Your will for me.

DECREE

I decree every satanic wall around my life is crashing down on the enemy's head. I declare God's Word breaks the enemy's plans as I speak it forth with authority, in Jesus's name.

Follow the Rules of Spiritual Warfare

There are rules of warfare against powers of darkness. One of the primary rules is "fear not." I have commanded you over and over again not to fear. The enemy smells fear. Fear attracts spiritual attacks because your opponent sees a weakness. You have absolutely no reason to fear. You have every reason to stand in faith. I am with you. I will not allow you to be defeated when you follow Me. Refuse to allow your flesh to dominate your spirit. Refuse to allow your soul to be intimidated. Look to Jesus, the author and finisher of your faith, and reject every notion of fear.

DEUTERONOMY 20:1; PSALM 56:3–4; PSALM 23:4

PRAYER

Father, help me fight according to the rules of engagement. Teach me how to fight Your way and win Your way, and I shall not fear.

DECREE

I decree fear, anxiety, dread, intimidation, and overwhelmed emotions infiltrate the enemy's camp. I declare the enemy's foul play will not stand up to my faith that overcomes, in Jesus's name.

October 13

Give Me Your Yes and Amen

Give me your yes and amen as I've given you My yes and amen, and together we will walk in places that eye has not seen, nor ear heard, nor have even entered into your heart—places the enemy has tried to prevent you from dreaming about. There are bountiful places for you. There are bountiful lands for you. There are bountiful blessings for you. With whom will you agree? With whom will you dream? Dream with Me, and I will dream with you.

2 CORINTHIANS 1:20; MATTHEW 5:37; 1 CHRONICLES 16:36

PRAYER

Father, I give you my yes and my amen. Help me believe Your yes and amen when the enemy is working on my mind to get me out of agreement with Your Spirit.

DECREE

I decree all alignment with the enemy of my soul is broken. I declare my eyes will see and my ears shall hear what God has planned for me in due season, in Jesus's name.

You Are Battle Ready

$\mathscr{I}$ have prepared your hands for battle and your fingers for war. I have given you strength to pull back the bow of bronze. I have made you able to run through a troop and leap over a wall. I have made you ready for the skirmishes, the confrontations, the run-ins, the battles, the onslaughts, and every form of enemy attack. You are well able, in the name of Jesus, to enforce the victory. I have given the enemy into your hands.

PSALM 144:1; PSALM 18:34; PROVERBS 21:31

PRAYER

Father, thank You for the seasons of preparation that brought me to this place of assured victory. Help me see the victory in every battle.

DECREE

I decree I am Christ's enforcer on the earth. I declare I am instant in season and out of season, ready for battle and fit for war against Kingdom foes, in Jesus's name.

October 15

I Am Giving You Grace to Resist

$\mathcal{M}$y grace is sufficient for you in every battle. There is grace to resist as you humble yourself to Me and acknowledge Me as King of kings, Lord of lords, and Warrior of warriors. Learn to tap into My grace. Learn how to appropriate My grace. You need to understand at a greater measure My grace. This word *grace* has been so abused in the body of Christ, and some have taken it to such extremes that few want to learn of it any longer. But My grace is still power, kindness, blessings, and favor. When the enemy of your soul is chasing you, remember My grace is in you.

2 CORINTHIANS 12:9; JAMES 4:6; HEBREWS 4:16

PRAYER

Father, teach me how to cooperate with Your saving grace, Your warring grace, and Your preserving grace. Help me rely on Your all-sufficient grace in every season.

DECREE

I decree great grace to disgrace and deface enemy powers follows me onto the battlefield. I declare God's grace is sufficient for every battle, in Jesus's name.

October 16

Pull the Tumbleweeds

$\mathcal{B}$egin to press deeper into My Word and allow it to sweep through the recesses of your soul and clear away the enemy's tumbleweeds. Tumbleweeds are not My will for you. I want you to be rooted and grounded in My love. I want you to be rooted and grounded in My Word. I want you to pull the weeds from the seeds the enemy planted to spoil the crop, to spoil the harvest, to spoil the peace, the truth, the deliverance, the freedom, the joy that I have for you.

2 TIMOTHY 3:16; LUKE 11:28; COLOSSIANS 3:16

PRAYER

Father, show me where the tumbleweeds are blowing through my soul to choke out Your Word so I can choose to choke them out of my life. Help me pull the weeds.

DECREE

I decree every demon power that sows tares in my soul is buried by his own schemes. I declare my mind is free from peace-killing weeds, in Jesus's name.

Surrender to the Author of Your Faith

*M*any in this season have surrendered their will to the enemy. Many in this season have surrender confused. You're not to raise a white flag in surrender to the wicked one. You are not to raise a white flag in surrender to the one who wants to kill, steal, and destroy you. But you are to surrender to Me, the author and the finisher of your faith, not the author and finisher of fear that seeks to destroy you. You are to surrender to Me.

MARK 14:35–36; ROMANS 12:1; PROVERBS 23:26

PRAYER

Father, I surrender to You and You alone. Help me see any areas of my life that are not fully surrendered to Your good, perfect, and acceptable will for my life.

DECREE

I decree my words of life author the enemy's utter defeat. I declare principalities pressuring my mind are bowing to the Price of Peace dwelling in my spirit.

October 18

Don't Give the Enemy a Second Thought

𝒟on't give the enemy's thoughts a second thought. Stop allowing the enemy to overtake your thoughts. Allow Me to overtake your thoughts. For My thoughts are higher than your thoughts, and they are certainly higher than the thoughts of the wicked one that you are allowing entrance into your soul. If you will allow My thoughts to be louder than your thoughts and the enemy's thoughts, you will see that your thinking level will bring a new Kingdom reality into your life because as a man thinks in his heart, so is he.

1 THESSALONIANS 5:21; PSALM 109:2–4; COLOSSIANS 2:8

PRAYER

Father, show me quickly when I start giving the enemy's thoughts a second, third, and fourth thought. Help me think of things that are good and pure and lovely.

DECREE

I decree the enemy's thought bombs are diffused and destroyed. I declare my thoughts are higher than the enemy's thoughts because I meditate on the Word, in Jesus's name.

October 19

Get Back to the Center

 I'm calling you back to the center because the enemy has tried to force you out of My presence. The enemy has tried to cause you to withdraw from My heart. I am calling you back to the center—out of the fringes and back to the center. This is where you will hear My heartbeat, and this is where you will see My face as you seek My face. This is where you will hear My voice and understand My will for your life. And you will see and know and understand that the attacks of the past season were to keep you out of this sweet spot—to keep you out of the next glory.

MATTHEW 6:33–34; EPHESIANS 5:15; MARK 6:31

PRAYER

Father, help me find my way back to the center of Your heart. Show me how to find balance in my day-to-day life so the enemy cannot devour me.

DECREE

I decree the fangs of the fierce demons threatening me are broken. I declare the attacks of the past season have taught me lessons of victory for the next, in Jesus's name.

Lift Your Voice to Heaven

*F*or the enemy is knock, knock, knocking on the door. The enemy is knock, knock, knock, knocking on the door of your mouth, and he is waiting for you to speak forth in agreement with what he whispered in your ear. Don't answer the door. Shout out My name. Sing out My praises. Lift up your voice to Heaven. Don't answer the door. Don't agree with your adversary in this way because he has come with an agenda of destruction. He wants to use you to destroy yourself. He doesn't have to do a thing, except get your yes.

PSALM 59:17; PSALM 142:1; PSALM 26:7

PRAYER

Father, when my throat is hoarse from shouting war cries and my mind is weary from the devil's constant knocking, help me drown out the enemy's voice with thoughts of You.

DECREE

I decree the angel of the Lord persecutes demon powers knocking on my door. I declare every door to my life is locked with the Word and sealed with the blood, in Jesus's name.

I Am Able to Make You Run

I will make the crooked places straight. I will make a table before you in the presence of your enemies, and they will see and know that the God in whom you trust has your back. They will see and know that the God in whom you believe has put you in a place of authority and a place of position, a place of power. For My Spirit dwells on the inside of you, and I am able to make you stand, and I am able to make you walk, and I am able to make you run, and I am able to make you win.

ISAIAH 45:2; PSALM 23:5; 2 SAMUEL 22:33–34

PRAYER

Father, make my legs strong and sturdy so I can run to the battle line, run to the finish line, and receive the crown of life. Help me to trust Your might inside my spirit.

DECREE

I decree crooked pathways thwart the entry of the enemy of my soul. I declare a table is set before the presence of my enemies and vindication is my portion, in Jesus's name.

October 22

When the Enemy Attacks You with Shame

*W*hen the enemy attacks you with shame, remember I've given You My name. I am your husbandman, and I will defend your honor and your name. I have marked you for greatness, and I have created you in My likeness. I am giving you grace to work out your salvation with fear and trembling. I am not ashamed of you. I accept you even as I am changing you from glory to glory. Shame the devil by celebrating who you are in Christ. Your past is gone. Your future is bright.

ISAIAH 61:7; ISAIAH 50:7; PSALM 31:17

PRAYER

Father, I put my full hope in You for every affair in my life, from my salvation to my identity in Christ to my victory in spiritual warfare. I trust in You.

DECREE

I decree the enemy working to publicly shame me is openly disgraced. I declare Christ already put the enemy to public shame and bore all my shame, in Jesus's name.

October 23

I Am Your Momentum

I am reminding you today that I am your momentum. I am your momentum in the battle, and I am your momentum in the good times. I am like the snowball effect in your life, and if you'll just cooperate with Me and not resist Me, if you'll just resist the devil and not resist Me, if you'll just submit to Me and not submit to the devil, if you'll just get your life in order with My Word, you will see in a moment that those things which had opposed you, year after year after year, will have to bow to you in My name because the momentum in your life will be so strong and be so great that it's almost unstoppable. Only you can stop it.

PHILIPPIANS 3:12–14; PSALM 92:12; JOHN 15:4

PRAYER

Father, help me submit to You fully so I can see the fullness of Your momentum in my life. Teach me to ride the wave of Your glory and the wind of Your Spirit.

DECREE

I decree deafness to every monitoring spirit that has come to spy on my momentum. I declare the enemy's momentum against is halted and reversed, in Jesus's name.

I Have an Oasis in the Desert

I have created an oasis in the midst of the desert. Find the oasis. Seek the oasis. Look for the oasis. It's not where you think. It's not behind you. It's in front of you. Keep on walking through the wilderness. I've not called you to camp out there. Keep on walking through the desert place. I've provided for you an oasis just like I provided for Hagar. Just like I would not allow her to die there, I will not allow you to die there. The enemy will not overcome you in the wilderness.

PSALM 107:35–36; HOSEA 13:5; GENESIS 21:8–21

PRAYER

Father, thank You for leading me and guiding me to a place of refreshing. Help me drink deep of Your love and Your peace when the pressure feels too great to stand.

DECREE

I decree every jackal spirit seeking to devour me is devoured by deep darkness. I declare I am walking through the wilderness to greater power, in Jesus's name.

Your Tongues Unlock Warfare Revelation

*W*hen you speak in a language that is even unknown to you—when you speak in your supernatural prayer language in the midst of the battle—you will be unlocking mysteries of warfare. You will gain revelation you can use as a weapon. You will see things and know things in your spirit that will come later as a revelation to your mind when you praise Me. Sing in the spirit. Sing the song of the Lord. Sing My Word. Sing My songs of victory even before you see the victory. Let your tongues bring revelation as you sing.

EPHESIANS 6:18; JUDE 20; ROMANS 8:26–27

PRAYER

Father, expand my heavenly prayer language to include words of war that release angels on assignment to combat the principalities and powers at work in my life.

DECREE

I decree tongues of fire burn up the enemy's fiery darts. I declare songs of deliverance echo over my life and overwhelm the enemy's ears, in Jesus's name.

Putting Thousands of Demons to Flight

I have called you not to fight every battle alone. I've called you to stand with others. For one can put one thousand to flight and two can put ten thousand to flight and together you will see swift victory. Stubborn battles that could not seem to be won will be won in an instant as you stand together in unity. For where there is unity, I command a blessing. That blessing is called victory, increase, retribution, and vindication. By allowing Me to use you as a war club for your brothers and sisters, I will bring increase to you, and the spoils of war will be part and in parcel of your reward.

1 PETER 3:8; 1 CORINTHIANS 1:10; PHILIPPIANS 2:2

PRAYER

Father, help me see any place of my mind that is not in unity with Your Spirit. Help me find those who can truly agree with me in spiritual warfare prayer unto victory.

DECREE

I decree a slippery path for the enemy trying to sneak up on my soul. I declare I am in unity with the body of Christ and the enemy is scurrying away, in Jesus's name.

October 27

You Have Choices to Make

$\mathscr{I}$ will not walk on you, but you can walk in Me. You can choose to rise above the pain and rise above the anger that you feel against the ones who took advantage of you over and over and over and over again. You can forgive those who walked on you and climbed over you to get where they wanted to go. You can choose to forgive. You can choose to rise up and war against the demon powers that are holding those in bondage that have wronged you. You can choose to act like the demon that inspired people to hurt you, or you can act like your Father who is in Heaven. The choice is yours.

DEUTERONOMY 30:19; LUKE 6:37; MATTHEW 5:48

PRAYER

Father, help me put on Christ and walk in Him every step of every day, and when I stumble looking at those who have hurt me, pick me back up again.

DECREE

I decree my enemies are like chaff before the wind and the angel of the Lord chases them out of my sight. I declare I love like my Father in Heaven, in Jesus's name.

Make Another Push

*R*ise up and birth now that which you failed to birth in the last season because of the weariness, because of the intensity of the attack, because of the atmospheric interference, and because of the mind traffic. Rise up and birth that which you couldn't push out in the last season because the battles in your soul caused you to think you weren't good enough, you weren't ready enough, you weren't strong enough. Make another push, and you will see that I am faithful to birth through you what I put in you. You can do this!

PHILIPPIANS 4:13; PSALM 20:8; PSALM 35:23

PRAYER

Father, give me the spiritual strength and the physical strength to fight another day. Break the weariness of my mind, will, emotions, and earthly frame.

DECREE

I decree my enemies collapse and fall, but I will rise up in the strength of the Lord. I declare I have the might to push back dark powers invading my space, in Jesus's name.

I've Given the Enemy into Your Hands

I've already given the enemy into your hands. All you have to do is believe. Walk in the way that I've called you to walk, to the places I've called you to walk, and out of the places I've called you to walk out of. Walk into My blessings, My anointing, My favor. My Spirit rests upon you. Do not allow yourself to be anxious, for you alone decide and determine how you feel and what you will meditate upon. The wicked one cannot control your mind. But you can. Stand with Me as I stand with you, and I will show you great and mighty things. If you can see the promise, you can have it. Only believe.

1 Samuel 24:4; Psalm 54; Psalm 63

PRAYER

Father, help me to control my mind, casting down imaginations, casting anxieties on You, casting my life into Your hands. I choose to believe Your promises.

DECREE

I decree a cease-and-desist order against every enemy operation in my life. I declare I see the promises of God and walk in them, in Jesus's name.

October 30

I Am About to Shoot You Forth

I'm about to restore you. I'm about to refresh you. I'm about to shoot you forward like an arrow. The enemy held you back for longer than you thought you could wait. The enemy hindered you at every turn so that everywhere you looked there was nothing but frustration. The enemy harassed you with wicked word bombs that aimed to blow up your faith. But you stayed the course. You didn't throw in the towel. The enemy pulled you back, but I am about to shoot you forth like an arrow that hits the mark.

PSALM 56:1; PSALM 35:1–9; 1 PETER 5:6

PRAYER

Father, harass those demon powers that harass me. Hinder those spirits that hinder Your will in my life. Help me walk in humility and wait for You to shoot me forth.

DECREE

I decree lightning and thunder into the path of harassing spirits. I declare God will shoot down enemy plans with His arrows of vengeance, in Jesus's name.

October 31

Burn and Shine

*M*y light is greater than deep darkness, than gross darkness, than the darkest of dark. My light will overcome any and every measure of darkness clouding your mind, your body, and your family. Let my light shine from within you, and you will blind the enemies of light. My light will illuminate your path and expose the enemy's darkness that aims to trip you up and slip you up. Jesus is the light of the world. Now, it's your turn. Burn and shine, and the enemy will flee.

JOHN 5:35; COLOSSIANS 1:3; PSALM 139:13

PRAYER

Father, I want to burn and shine for You. Baptize me with fire, and I will expose gross darkness with the light of Your gospel. I will be Your witness in the earth.

DECREE

I decree the eyes of the enemy peering into my life are blinded by the light of God within me. I declare God's light leads and guides me out of enemy shadows, in Jesus's name.

NOVEMBER

See that no one renders evil for evil to anyone, but always pursue what is good both for yourselves and for all. Rejoice always, pray without ceasing, in everything give thanks; for this is the will of God in Christ Jesus for you. Do not quench the Spirit.

1 THESSALONIANS 5:15–19

The War for Your Harvest

*A*s long as the earth remains, there will be seedtime and harvesttime. If you want a harvest, you must sow a seed. If you want a generous harvest, you must sow a generous seed. For he who sows sparingly reaps sparingly, but he who sows generously reaps generously. But watch your seed. Water it with the word of your mouth. Don't curse your seed in the ground. Don't let the enemy choke the seed with faithless words from your heart. Believe Me for the harvest.

GENESIS 8:22; 2 CORINTHIANS 9:10; PSALM 65:11

PRAYER

Father, help me speak life over the seed You lead me to sow in the ground. Help me not to eat my seed, curse my seed, or pull my seed up before the harvest.

DECREE

I decree every seed I plant in the ground brings forth maximum blessing. I declare God watches over His Word I speak from my mouth to perform it, in Jesus's name.

Change Your Spiritual Diet

Stop eating the enemy's food. Stop chewing on the demonic thoughts he whispers that make your stomach sick and your head hurt. Stop eating the enemy's portion. Your portion is not bitterness. Your portion is not pain. Your portion is not unforgiveness. Your portion is not fear. Your portion is not rejection. Instead, taste and see that I am good. Eat My Word. The words I have left you are spirit and life. They are like honey to your lips. It's time to change your spiritual diet.

EZEKIEL 3:3; PSALM 34:8; 1 PETER 2:3

PRAYER

Father, help me develop a taste for the things You love and a distaste for the things You hate. Help me to speak words that bring sweet life to bitter warfare.

DECREE

I decree the toxic scrolls the enemy has tried to feed me will poison his own pot. I declare the enemy will not force-feed me bitter realities, but I will eat the Word, in Jesus's name.

Agree with My Victory

*D*on't be defeated. Don't be discouraged in your own mind. Don't be defeated in your own heart. Don't buy into the enemies' lies. You cannot lose. I said you cannot lose. Agree with Me and not with your adversary. Come into union with Me. Get into unity with My heart for what I have in store for your life. Don't agree with the enemy. Don't agree with the mockers. Don't agree with the naysayers. Don't agree with those who don't agree with Me. How can two walk together unless they agree? Walk with Me and agree with Me.

AMOS 3:3; GALATIANS 6:7; MATTHEW 18:19

PRAYER

Father, help me come into true agreement with Your Word and Your specific will for my life so the enemy cannot move me from the stance of truth and patience.

DECREE

I decree any and all agreements, casual covenants, and contracts I have made with the enemy are broken. I declare I walk in the statutes of God, in Jesus's name.

Don't Listen to the Critics

Don't say about yourself negative things people say about you. What do they know? Say about yourself what I say about you. I am your Creator. I know you intimately. The power of life and death is in your tongue. Don't think about what they're thinking about you. Think about what I'm thinking about you. What I think about you is all that matters, and I'm thinking good thoughts toward you. I've got great and mighty exploits for you to do. What I think and say about you is in My Word and in My heart. Don't listen to the critics. Listen to me.

PROVERBS 22:10; PSALM 1:1; DANIEL 11:32

PRAYER

Father, help me to maintain my identity in the face of scoffers, mockers, and haters who want to tear me down. Help me to think of myself the way You think of me.

DECREE

I decree demons conspiring against me to criticize and mock me are muted. I declare I am who God says I am, and I can do what God says I can do, in Jesus's name.

Rely On My Wisdom for the Battle

*R*emember, your victory is not by your might, not by your power, but by My spirit. Don't try to take on the enemy in your own wisdom, your own strength, or even with the strategy of your last battle. You will win this war by wearing My armor, by wielding My weapons, and by following My Spirit. I will always lead you into triumph when you follow Me and do things My way. Don't rely on your own power and might. Rely on Mine.

ZECHARIAH 4:6; EPHESIANS 6:12; 2 CORINTHIANS 10:4

PRAYER

Father, help me not to fight with my own strength, my own armor, and my own weapons. Teach me to rely on You when I want to run ahead without You.

DECREE

I decree the enemy's weapons of warfare are weak and ineffectual against the name, the Word, and the blood. I declare I walk in God's wisdom for warfare, in Jesus's name.

I Am the Warrior of Warriors

*Y*ou've heard it said Jesus is the King of kings and the Lord of lords. You've heard it said, "The Lord is a warrior, the Lord is His name." I am indeed a warrior. I fight darkness with light and fight hate with truth. You are a warrior in Me, the great I Am, the greater One Who not only lives on the inside of you but trains your spirit for battle. You war from a position of the warrior's victory on the cross. Your faith in My ability in you will give you the victory. This is the victory that overcomes the world, even your faith. Now war, warrior!

EXODUS 15:3; ISAIAH 42:13; JEREMIAH 31:35

PRAYER

Father, help me see myself as a warrior in Christ. Help me understand the greater warrior on the inside of me has armed me for victory.

DECREE

I decree the warrior in me overshadows the enemy's war against me. I declare my position is victory before, during, and after every battle, in Jesus's name.

You Are Not a Victim

*Y*ou are not a victim. You are a victor. And even though the enemy has victimized you, even though the enemy has terrorized you, even though the enemy has even made you feel at times like you are losing your mind, there is payback and there is sevenfold return and even more so as you follow Me. I won't just give you double for your trouble; I won't just give you triple for your trial, but I will give you sevenfold as a minimum return on the investment that you made in trying to do My will and not understanding fully yet how to fight the wicked one.

DEUTERONOMY 20:4; PSALM 20:5; PSALM 21

PRAYER

Father, give me the sevenfold return on what the enemy stole as a demonstration of Your justice and Your goodness. Empower me to take back what belongs to me.

DECREE

I decree double for my trouble, triple for my trial, and a sevenfold return. I declare compounded compound interest on everything the enemy stole, in Jesus's name.

You Can Outwit Your Adversary

The enemy is fierce, but I am fiercer—and you are fierce in Me. I have created you with a fierce mind that is able to endure the incessant enemy attacks through subtle whispers. I have created you with a sensitive heart to hear My voice and shift your battle plans on a moment's notice to outwit your adversary. I have created you with a desire and a mandate for victory, not just for yourself but for the underdogs around you. Begin to see yourself as fierce. Begin to see yourself as victorious. Begin to see yourself as I see you. You are strong in Me and the power of My might.

Exodus 23:22; Numbers 10:9; Deuteronomy 32:41

PRAYER

Father, let Your voice be the loudest one I hear when demonic winds are blowing against my life. Help me to see myself as fierce just as You are fierce.

DECREE

I decree the adversary of my life is outwitted by the manifold wisdom of God. I declare I am fierce in the Lord and the fire of God consumes my enemies, in Jesus's name.

Repentance Will Bring Victory

Repentance is part of your warfare. Don't enter the raging war without repenting of your sins and asking Me to forgive you of all unrighteousness. Don't go into the battle with unforgiveness in your heart. Don't release your war cry until you release the cry of repentance. Don't let the devil get an advantage over you by neglecting to allow Me to wash you with the water of My Word and cleanse you with the blood of the Lamb. Check your heart before you rush in with spiritual guns blazing.

ISAIAH 30:15; JEREMIAH 31:9; HOSEA 4:12

PRAYER

Father, I repent for being undone by the enemy's attacks. I repent for any area of disobedience that opened the door for the wicked one to harass me.

DECREE

I decree repentance is my warfare and releases me from the enemy's snare. I declare my spiritual guns blaze against the dark forces working to tempt me, in Jesus's name.

November 10

Trade the Cares for Prayers

*C*ast your cares on Me because I care for you. My yoke is easy, and My burden is light. My commandments are not burdensome. Stop taking on the cares of all those around you. Begin to lift up prayers instead of taking on cares. I have all wisdom and I reign supreme over the enemy and I am able to work these things out for your good and for those who you love. I am able to do more than you can think or imagine. If you'll just believe Me, you will release the cares to Me and begin to pray instead of weep and cry and feel anxious and overwhelmed and stressed out.

PSALM 13:2; PSALM 55:22; MATTHEW 27:43

PRAYER

Father, I trade my cares for prayers. Help me truly release the burdens of my heart into Your capable hands so the enemy cannot choke Your Word out of my heart.

DECREE

I decree the enemy must choke on the lies with which he is trying to choke me. I declare my faith and hope is in God, Who will deliver me out of all my cares, in Jesus's name.

I Will Bring You to the Point of Breakthrough

*W*eeping may endure for a night, but joy comes in the morning. For I am with you to gather up your tears from the enemy attacks, the hurts, and the wounds. I've kept them in a bottle. And I will come to comfort you by My Spirit. Keep looking at Me, and little by little I will heal you from the trauma of the warfare and the losses. Little by little I will make the wrong things right. Little by little I will bring you to the point of breakthrough where the past really is the past and the future looks bright.

PSALM 30:5; PSALM 56:8; PSALM 126:5

PRAYER

Father, help me enter into Your presence so I can find fullness of joy and enter into the breakthrough You have prepared for me. Clear my eyes of tears.

DECREE

I decree the enemy of my soul is persecuted with God's tempest. I declare weeping may endure for a season, but the joy of the Lord is my portion and strength, in Jesus's name.

Be Careful How You Listen

*B*e careful how you listen. The enemy will always lead you and guide you into lies, deception, self-pity, evil thoughts about others, and dark imaginations. The Holy Spirit will lead you and guide you into all truth. Study My Word. My Word is truth. My Word expresses My will for your life. My Word is purified by fire seven times. The enemy's words will set your life on hellfire if you let them. You have to make a decision today whose voice you are going to listen to. There are many voices in the spirit world and none without significance. Allow the voice of My Word to take the place of significance in your life and listen well. I love you.

JOHN 16:13; PROVERBS 1:5; PROVERBS 22:17

PRAYER

Father, help me incline my ear to You and not to the voice of the wicked one so I can hear words of life that build faith to conquer every mountain and every demon.

DECREE

I decree the enemy who has taken crafty counsel against me must bow to the counsel of the Lord. I declare God's voice rings in my spirit and guides me, in Jesus's name.

I Am the Breaker

*F*ierce has been the battle against you, and great has been the oppression upon you. But I am the breaker, and I go before you. If you will follow Me out of the place you stand, I will take you beyond into a new season of victory. I will take you beyond into a new season of provision because there is increase that has already been laid aside for you. Your inheritance and your portion are secure. The enemy has not devoured that which I have called you to and planned for you, but you can rise up and regain what was lost with interest.

MICAH 2:13; 1 CHRONICLES 14:11; PSALM 71:21

PRAYER

Father, thank You for sending Jesus, the breaker, to make a way for my breakthrough. Help me to follow You into new dimensions of victory I haven't seen before.

DECREE

I decree the confederate that has risen against me is like stubble before the wind. I declare the enemy's plans are broken to bits by the Breaker, in Jesus's name.

Don't Buy Into the Enemy's Story Line

*E*ven though the enemy is pressuring you and pounding on your mind—even though it feels like the enemy has knocked the wind out of you—walk by faith and not by feelings. Know that I am breathing on you even now. I am releasing the winds of refreshing in this season of constriction. You will see. You will come to know, and you will firmly believe the enemy's constriction is merely fiction. It's just smoke and mirrors. It's just a mirage. It's just a bunch of circumstantial evidence. It's not real, it's false evidence appearing real. Don't buy into the enemy's story line. My Word is truth.

PSALM 55:1–3; MATTHEW 7:14; ROMANS 5:3

PRAYER

Father, help me catch my breath when it feels like the wind has escaped my lungs. Help me follow Your story line for my life and rewrite the enemy's tragic plot.

DECREE

I decree the enemy is convicted for foul play and cannot rewrite my future. I declare God's plans are to give me a good future and hope, in Jesus's name.

The Enemy Attack Is Temporary

*W*hen fear rises against you, when rejection hits your mind, when natural circumstances worry you, when chaos and confusion and drama and sorrow and grief stir like a whirlwind in your soul, remember this: these feelings are only as real as you allow it to be. I am more real than your circumstances. Your circumstances are temporary. Your emotions are temporary. The enemy's attack is temporary. I am eternal. I am the greater One. My Spirt lives on the inside of you to empower you to overcome the fear, rejection, chaos, confusion, worry, drama, sorrow, and grief. Now, say "Peace be still" to your soul and send the enemy packing.

2 CORINTHIANS 4:17–18; DANIEL 7:14; 2 CORINTHIANS 5:1

PRAYER

Father, help me remember Your precious words to me. They are like honey to my soul in a time of famine. Help me see that this too shall pass.

DECREE

I decree the wrath of God is pouring out on eternal enemies who seek my destruction. I declare my suffering for Christ's sake releases glory over me, in Jesus's name.

Hope Fuels Your Faith to Fight

I'm setting you up for success. I'm setting you up for breakthrough. I'm setting you up to see those things that I spoke to you about in the last season. All My promises are yes and amen. The enemy has interrupted your hope. The enemy has tried to constrict you, tried to squeeze you, tried to wear you out and run you down. The enemy has tried to force your hand and convince you to give up. But he cannot force My hand, and I haven't given up. So, get up and fight. Get up and swing the sword I have given you. Choose to believe that the next season will be greater than the last season. Choose to hope again. Hope gives you fuel to fight the good fight of faith.

ROMANS 15:13; PSALM 39:7; PSALM 71:5

PRAYER

Father, renew my hope, and it will fuel my faith. Give me a fresh perspective on my situation so I can hope again when the warfare has made my heart sick.

DECREE

I decree the enemy's plots toward me are hopeless and failing. I declare my new season is before me, and I am following the Holy Spirit through the door, in Jesus's name.

Don't Tie My Hands

*L*et me deal with your persecutors. Let me deal with your detractors. Let me deal with your abusers. Don't you do it. Take your hands off this. I will vindicate you. Take your mouth off them. I will show them to be in the wrong. Don't tie my hands with a vengeance mind-set. Vengeance is mine. I will repay. I know it's tempting. I know your flesh rises up when you see their success at your expense. Let My Spirit rise up and defend you. Let Me make it right for you. Your payback is in Me. Let's do this My way. My ways are higher than your ways. Trust Me.

PSALM 42:4–8; ISAIAH 50:8; PSALM 26:1

PRAYER

Father, deal with my persecutors. Show mercy on them. Bless them with spiritual blessings. Give them a revelation of Your great love. Forgive them.

DECREE

I decree the vengeance of God falls now on the enemies of my soul. I declare demon powers are subject to me and payback belongs to me, in the name of Jesus.

When the Enemy Tries to Shake Your Faith

I see the enemy trying to move you off the position of faith. Stand firm. Stand strong knowing that whatever can be shaken will be shaken—but you shall not be moved when you trust in Me. I've got you in My hands, and I'm able to make you stand in the evil day. I'm able to make you stand in the midst of the battle. I'm able to make you stand when all hell is breaking loose against you. I am able to make you stand. Don't bow down to the imaginations in your mind. Bow down to Me. Don't bow to the spirit of fear. Don't bow to that spirit of discouragement. Bow to Me.

PSALM 69:23; PSALM 125:5–7; PSALM 16:8

PRAYER

Father, make me stand amid the shaking all around me. When the enemy tries to shake me up, help me shake it off and keep on standing in Your will.

DECREE

I decree the tongue of discouraging demons is tied in unsolvable knots. I declare my enemies are shaken out and exposed by the light of God, in Jesus's name.

When the Enemy Comes Knocking

*W*hen I come knocking on your door, you will feel a peace and you will feel a joy. You will not feel fear, but you will feel contentment and satisfaction. You will feel an expectation and an exhilaration. When the enemy comes knocking on your door you will feel dread. You will feel fear. You will feel confusion. You will feel trepidation. When I come knocking, open up to Me and sup with Me, dine with Me, fellowship with Me, with My heart, with My Spirit. For I have called you into a secret place where the enemy cannot find. But you must enter in through my door.

PSALM 91:1; ISAIAH 44:2; 1 CORINTHIANS 14:33

PRAYER

Father, help me discern the enemy's knock on the door of my heart from Your knock. Help me to lock it up when the devil tries to knock it down.

DECREE

I decree evil shall hunt my violent enemies and overthrow them. I declare the enemy can't find me hiding in the secret place reserved for me, in Jesus's name.

I Will Give You Wisdom for the Warfare

I will give you wisdom for the warfare. And I will give you an understanding of the attack, the root causes, and the issues that have left you in this place feeling unable to fight. Be confident in this: I am able to make you fight. I am not just able to make you stand; I am able to make you fight. I am able to cause increase in your life as you sow My Word into your heart, despite the warfare that is coming against you. Don't stop sowing My Word. Don't stop speaking My Word. Don't stop warring with My Word because these things are guaranteed to work for you in any battle.

PSALM 19:7; PSALM 73:24; PSALM 147:5

PRAYER

Father, give me wisdom. Help me tap into Your limitless wisdom so I can overcome the wisdom of the world and the wisdom of the devil. Make me wise.

DECREE

I decree bloodthirsty demons are rooted out and routed. I declare the wisdom of demons can't combat God's wisdom operating in my life, in Jesus's name.

I Am Sharpening You

$\mathscr{I}$ am indeed sharpening you. I'm sharpening you with My words, and I'm sharpening you by My Spirit. I'm putting you in the company of other spiritual warriors, where iron sharpens iron, and you will sharpen one another. Don't run and isolate yourself when the warfare hits, but instead run to the company of other people who know how to fight and let them sharpen you. Let them stand with you and you stand with them. Sharpen each other with My Word.

PROVERBS 27:17; EPHESIANS 6:13; ECCLESIASTES 10:10

PRAYER

Father, sharpen me with Your Word. Send people in my path who can sharpen me and who I can sharpen so that together we can overtake the wicked one's schemes.

DECREE

I decree the tongues of the divisive are divided and ineffective. I declare I am sharp and growing sharper as my mind is renewed by the Word that's a sword, in Jesus's name.

Run to the Throne

*R*un to My throne of grace when you fall to the enemy's temptation. My throne is a throne of grace. My throne is a throne of mercy. The foundation of My throne is righteousness and justice. Run to my throne even when you fall to fear, fall to unbelief, or fall to sin. You can approach My throne any time to find grace and obtain mercy to help in a time of need—any need. You can come to Me at any moment with faith that I will receive you. I am here for you. Don't run from Me when you are overwhelmed, when you lose hope, when you feel condemned. Run to my throne. I will not forsake you.

HEBREWS 4:16; REVELATION 2:20; PSALM 103:9

PRAYER

Father, give me the strength to run to Your throne to obtain grace and mercy to help in a time of need. I need Your revelation. Receive my desperate prayer.

DECREE

I decree the enemies around God's throne accusing me day and night are condemned. I declare the courts of Heaven rule in my favor by the blood, in Jesus's name.

Take Responsibility

*N*o one can fight your battles for you. You have to rise up and fight. Yes, my heavenly host will back you up at My command. Yes, I will sometimes choose to send intercessors to cover you in prayer in the heat of the battle. Yes, I will send faithful ones to lift up your arms when you grow too weary. But ultimately you have to run to the battle line. You have to be willing to get in the fight. You have to take on the enemies that attack your mind. You have to take responsibility.

GALATIANS 6:5; EZRA 10:4; 1 TIMOTHY 6:12

PRAYER

Father, I hear Your Word, and I will rise up and fight as You strengthen me to engage in the battle. Make me willing to fight when I am too weary to dress for battle.

DECREE

I decree demons are ashamed and confounded that seek after my soul. I declare all of Heaven is for me as I run to the battle line, in Jesus's name.

Use Thanksgiving as a Weapon

The enemy will tempt you to complain about the territorial warfare for My will, but I am calling you to maintain and take new ground for my Kingdom. The enemy will lure you into self-pity, mumbling, groaning, and looking back at what you see as a better life. But I have given you thanksgiving as a weapon to plow through the enemy's tactics that tempt you to question Me, accuse Me, and leave Me out of the battle plans. Use thanksgiving as a weapon to cut through the enemy's doubt. Your words have power.

PSALM 107:1; PSALM 100:4; PSALM 50:14

PRAYER

Father, remind me to give You thanks in the midst of the battle, even when defeat appears to be my portion. Stir me to thank You for the victory in advance.

DECREE

I decree lying tongues that tempt me to accuse God are cut off. I declare my God is faithful to bring me into the promises He swore in His Word, in Jesus's name.

When You're Facing Unrelenting Warfare

*W*hen you can no longer hold on to your spiritual sword and you can no longer hold on to your shield of faith, hold on to Me because I am holding on to you. Hold on to Me, and I will carry you to a resting place. Just hold My hand, and I will walk you around the landmines. Just hold on to Me, and I will bring you to a place of new strength and peace in the midst of the unrelenting warfare. I am the strength of your life, of whom shall you be afraid. Hold on to Me.

PSALM 6:2; PSALM 73:26; ISAIAH 35:3

PRAYER

Father, strengthen me because my heart has grown weak from the incessant attacks of the wicked ones. My bones feel weak, and my soul is dry. Help me rise again.

DECREE

I decree the cords of the wicked wrapped around my life are cut asunder. I declare new strength is my portion, and weakness fades away from my soul, in Jesus's name.

Let the Blindside Open Your Eyes

*A*t times the enemy blindsides you. You just didn't see it coming because you were looking at a false flag. But a blindside will open your eyes to the tactics of the enemy and make you wiser if you'll let it. Don't look at this battle from the eyes of failure. Don't look at this battle from the eyes of defeat. Learn the lesson in the loss. Remember that the enemy will use whatever he can to distract you from his work so that you don't notice him coming. Stay alert in the Spirit. You'll see it next time.

PSALM 4:8; LUKE 21:34; MATTHEW 24:43

PRAYER

Father, help me correct my warfare vision so I can see the enemy coming from far off and from nearby, from the front, the back, and the side. Help me learn and grow.

DECREE

I decree the enemy of my soul is distracted and falls on his own sword. I declare distractions have no attraction for me, and I am watchful at all times, in Jesus's name.

I Will Give You Rest from Your Enemies

Come to Me all of you who are weary and burdened and overwhelmed, and I, Myself, will give you rest for your souls, rest for your bodies, rest on all sides, and even rest from your enemies. I will hide you under the shadow of My wings. You will be protected in My presence. Come away with Me. Step out of the battlefield and walk with Me beside still waters. My rod and My staff will comfort you. You will find strength to reenter the fight. Wait upon Me, and I will renew your strength for the war you find yourself in.

1 KINGS 5:4; JOSHUA 21:44; PSALM 147:14

PRAYER

Father, protect me in Your presence. As I draw near to You, draw near to me and strengthen me for the next round of this wrestling match.

DECREE

I decree the desires of the wicked for my life are derailed by God's desires. I declare God is the strength of my life and He walks with me and talks with me, in Jesus's name.

Lean into My Purifying Fire

As hot as the fiery trial is upon you, that is how hot the fire of My presence will be in your life. My enemy's fire sets your life on hell, but My fire will cause you to burn and shine for Me. It's going to be worth it. Resist the enemy's fire but submit to My fire. Yield to Me. You won't even have to decide what to let go and what to blot out, because I, Myself, will burn it away. Resist the enemy's fire, but don't resist My fire. Discern the difference. Lean into My purifying fire, and the enemy will have less in you to work with.

PSALM 19:12; PSALM 51:7; JOHN 17:17

PRAYER

Father, I choose by my will to lean into Your purifying fire. I submit to the Spirit of burning and welcome the coal of fire to my mouth to purge and cleanse me.

DECREE

I decree agents of darkness plotting against me are cast into the fire that they may not rise up against me again. I declare God's fire is greater than enemy fire, in Jesus's name.

I Saw the Enemy Knock You Down—Get Up

I see how the enemy knocked you down. Beloved, get up. If you will try, My grace will meet you where you are and take you to a place where I want you to be. Get up. Stop looking at all the things that caused you to fall down—even the self-condemnation, guilt, shame, and accusations of the enemy. I am not accusing you, beloved. The condemnation is not coming from Me. I love you. I am for you, not against you. I am the one who will redeem and restore and reconcile. You have to get up now. You've laid there long enough. You've watched things waste away long enough.

PSALM 7:6; PSALM 119:62; PSALM 37:4

PRAYER

Father, You see all things, and You know all things. Help me not condemn myself because I didn't see it coming, because I didn't hear You warning me of the attack.

DECREE

I decree wicked devices of enemies who have exalted themselves against me are cut off. I declare the waste places in my life are restored, in Jesus's name.

Your Stumbling Will Turn into Soaring

*A*lthough you stumbled over your own self, although you stumbled over your own flesh, although the enemy was able to use your own mind against you, I have not called you to lick your wounds. I have not called you to look backward because hindsight may be 20/20, but I am able to give you a vision that is perfect, a vision that is reaching far into your future to inspire you because My hope for you, My future for you, it is good and it has not changed. Your stumbling is turning into soaring.

PSALM 56:13; JOB 4:4; PSALM 116:8

PRAYER

Father, help me get over myself so I can do Your will. Give me eyes to see in the spirit and strength to soar into my future, and I will glorify Your name.

DECREE

I decree stumbling blocks into the path of the enemy who is trying to cause me to stumble. I declare my stumbling will turn into soaring as I look at God, in Jesus's name.

DECEMBER

And war broke out in heaven: Michael and his angels fought with the dragon; and the dragon and his angels fought, but they did not prevail, nor was a place found for them in heaven any longer. So the great dragon was cast out, that serpent of old, called the Devil and Satan, who deceives the whole world; he was cast to the earth, and his angels were cast out with him. Then I heard a loud voice saying in heaven, "Now salvation, and strength, and the kingdom of our God, and the power of His Christ have come, for the accuser of our brethren, who accused them before our God day and night, has been cast down."

REVELATION 12:7–10

Let Me Carry Your War Burdens

*Y*our load will be a little lighter if you'll let Me take it off your shoulders. I can carry your burdens and carry you too. Let Me help you in this battle. You'll begin to walk a little faster without those heavy weights, then you'll begin to run again and see the progress you've been hoping to see—the progress you've been frustrated that you haven't seen. You'll be stronger to fight the wars that I've called you to fight if you'll lean into My grace and My wisdom. You don't have to go it alone. Remember, I am a very present help in time of need.

MATTHEW 11:28; HEBREWS 12:1; PSALM 46:1

PRAYER

Father, remove the heavy weights of oppression the enemy has fastened around my feet so I can run to the battle line with confidence and overcome the wicked one.

DECREE

I decree the wisdom of the God confounds every foe that stands against His will for my life. I declare My Helper stands by me in every battle I am called to fight, in Jesus's name.

Your Discernment Is Sharper

You didn't always know how to fight, but I've been teaching your hands to battle and your fingers to war. You didn't always know how to fight, but I've made your arms strong so you can bend a bow of steel. You didn't always know how to fight, but you've learned a lot since the last battle. You've been growing in My grace, little by little, from glory to glory. You are stronger now, and you are able to go back and take what the devil stole. You are able to see what you couldn't see before. You are able to discern what you didn't discern before. You are understanding and knowing things that you just had no clue about before.

PSALM 144:1; PSALM 18:34; PROVERBS 18:15

PRAYER

Father, teach me to fight like one of David's mighty men so that I can single-handedly plow through every oppressive thought and take the plunder.

DECREE

I decree the hands of demons weighing out violence against me are bound. I declare I see clearly into the spirit realm, discern and break attacks against me, in Jesus's name.

Disrupt the Disrupters

*I*t's time to disrupt the disrupters. You've tolerated enemy disruptions long enough. You have to take a stand against harassing spirits. You have to bind hindering spirits. You have to come against spirits that distract you from your calling and your purpose. You have to do this. I've given you the authority to bind and loose. I've given you dominion in the earth. I've given you the weapons of warfare, the armor of God in the name of Jesus. Don't stand by and watch as the enemy works his ministry in your life. Disrupt the disrupters.

GALATIANS 5:7; 1 THESSALONIANS 2:18; GENESIS 1:26–28

PRAYER

Father, forgive me for tolerating the work of the enemy in my life. Strengthen me to stand against harassing spirits that hinder Your plans for me in this season.

DECREE

I decree disruptions into the enemy's functions. I declare the enemy's ministry to my mind is shut down, and I receive the ministry of Holy Spirit, in Jesus's name.

You Will Plunder the Enemy's Camp

I will lead you into the enemy's camp to take back what was stolen at the *kairos* time. Don't rush against the enemy with fleshy anger. Wait on Me to lead you in triumphant battle. Like David at Ziklag, ask Me, "Shall I go up?" I will empower you to plunder the enemy's camp and take back what he stole from you and even more so. But wait on Me. I gave an opportune time in mind for this spiritual warfare campaign. Wait on Me.

1 SAMUEL 30:26; 1 SAMUEL 30:6

PRAYER

Father, empower me to plunder the enemy's camp after the disappointment of grave losses. Teach me to encourage myself in the Lord like David did.

DECREE

I decree the wealth of the riches has been stored up for the righteous. I declare the plunder I take back from the enemy's camp is so great that I have to sow into the lives of many, in Jesus's name.

December 5

New Strategies to Fight Old Enemies

 I will give you new strategies to fight the old enemies. Your enemies will always come back at what appears to be an opportune time, to kick you when you are down, to pile on when you feel like you can't take anymore. But I will show you with pinpoint accuracy how to defeat the old enemy that lurks in wait for the right moment to attack. Draw near to Me, and I will show you what is lurking and how to defend against it. You will send those old enemies packing, just like you did last time.

LUKE 4:13; 2 CORINTHIANS 2:11; EPHESIANS 4:27

PRAYER

Father, You are the master strategist. Help me incline my ear to hear Your strategy so I can swiftly conquer the enemies of Your will in my life.

DECREE

I decree the arrow from my quiver hits the enemy in the heart and forces him to flee. I declare every old enemy is intimidated by the God inside me, in Jesus's name.

Disrupting the Devil's Financial Delays

Sometimes you have to sow a disruptive seed. You need to break the rhythm of your giving. If you sow the same seed all the time, you will get the same harvest. A disruptive seed will break the cycle and break you into levels of harvest. When you sow a disruptive seed by the leading of My Spirit, you are disrupting the enemy's plans to spoil your harvest. When you obey Me and sow a disruptive seed, you are disrupting your natural resources and unlocking supernatural resources.

MARK 12:41–44; MALACHI 3:8–12; 2 CORINTHIANS 9:6

PRAYER

Father, help me break demonic cycles over my economy. Show me how my seed unlocks supernatural resources and shuts out enemy influences.

DECREE

I decree the devil's operations against my finances are disrupted and dismantled. I declare my disruptive seed yields an innovative harvest, in Jesus's name.

Discern the Onslaught

*Y*ou won't defeat the onslaught if you don't discern it. If you think you are just having a bad day, a bad week, or a bad month but neglect to use the powers of discernment within you to recognize cycles, patterns, and circles the enemy has you running in, you won't resist. You'll just think you are having a bad day, a bad week, or a bad month. When all hell is breaking lose against you, stop and pray. Discern the onslaught and you can break the cycle.

1 JOHN 2:27; 1 KINGS 3:9; HEBREWS 5:14

PRAYER

Father, help me discern the onslaught. Help me avoid soulish reasoning over the spiritual warfare that's raging against me and discern the spirits behind it.

DECREE

I decree a torrent of God's fury over the agents of onslaught operating in violence against my life. I decree the cycle is broken, in Jesus's name.

December 8

Newfound Faith for Payback

I know you feel as if you've lost a lot to the hand of the enemy. Stop looking at what you've lost with hopeless eyes and look at what you've lost through the eyes of My recompense. Then rise up and determine in your heart to count both sides of the cost. Just as you counted the cost before you went to war, count the cost of what you lost in the battles of the past. I will avenge you, and I will repay you with interest. You need to do your part. You need to be willing to rise up and swing the sword again with newfound faith for a payback.

JOB 42:10; ZECHARIAH 9:12; PROVERBS 6:31

PRAYER

Father, help me do my part. Help me be willing to rise up and fight again after so many setbacks. Give me a determination to war for the payback You have ordained.

DECREE

I decree the enemies of my destiny are cast into deep pits of destruction. I declare my faith is strong and getting stronger as I walk in God's perspective, in Jesus's name.

Banish the Demonic Creepers

Stop allowing the demonic creepers into your life. Sometimes these demonic voices creep in unaware. The voice of fear creeps in disguised as reasoning. The voice of offense creeps in on the back of pride. Sometimes creepers don't disguise themselves at all. Creepers like condemnation have a loud, bold voice. Creepers like guilt and shame are vocal about who you are not and what you'll never be. Stop giving ear to the creepers. Cast them out and listen to My voice. Be aware of My voice and let it be the loudest that you hear.

ROMANS 8:1; PROVERBS 22:10; JEREMIAH 33:3

PRAYER

Father, help me discern demons creeping in to spy out my liberty and take me captive to vain imaginations. Help me turn a deaf ear to the demonic chatter accusing me.

DECREE

I decree every disguised enemy is exposed and evicted from my presence. I declare I am aware and alert in the spirit at all times, in Jesus's name.

Releasing Divine Arrows from Heaven

Demonic fiery darts are no match for divine arrows from Heaven. I have given you the shield to quench every single flaming missile the enemy throws your way. But I have also given you divine arrows of deliverance to shoot at the heart of the enemy's plans to put you and keep you in bondage. I have given you strength to bend a bow of bronze. Remember, the battle is ultimately Mine, and I will use My own arrows against the onslaught if I need to. Trust in Me.

2 KINGS 13:17; PSALM 18:34; DEUTERONOMY 32:23

PRAYER

Father, release Your divine arrows into the enemy's camp and cut through the confusion he is releasing at my mind. Remind me to cry out for Your deliverance swiftly.

DECREE

I decree divine arrows from Heaven pierce the darkness over my life with glorious light. I declare God's arrows overtake demonic arrows flying at me, in Jesus's name.

I Will Give You Words to War With

*W*hen people curse and judge you, I will give you the right words to say—or help you not to say anything at all. I will give you the right words to war with in the spirit realm to combat the enemy assignment against your integrity and your identity. I will give you the right words to sing, and your praises will act as a weapon of confusion targeting the enemy's camp. I will put a new song in your mouth—songs of war and songs of deliverance—and your praise will abolish the enemy's plans for your life. Sing My praises. Speak My words.

PSALM 137:6; EXODUS 23:27; PSALM 55:9–15

PRAYER

Father, help me remain quiet when You don't want me to defend myself. Help me sing a song of praise instead of lifting a complaint about injustice.

DECREE

I decree my words are like weapons that strike down the enemy's assignment against me. I declare those who curse me are exposed as erroneous, in Jesus's name.

This Revelation Will Inspire You to Fight

*W*ake up the mighty men. Gather the soldiers. Discuss the strategies of war within the presence of My Spirit. Get in agreement and stand in unity one with another. When you do, I will pour out revelation upon you. This revelation will sharpen you. This revelation will inform you of the enemy's plans. This revelation will inspire you to fight the good fight. This revelation will cause you to soar higher in the spirit, up and above the warfare.

JOEL 3:9; EPHESIANS 1:17; PSALM 133

PRAYER

Father, wake me up and take me up in the spirit. Help me not to sleep and slumber, giving opportunity for the enemy to sow seeds that yield a wicked harvest in my life.

DECREE

I decree the enemy's onslaught backfires on his heinous hierarchy of demons because I am determined to see God's will. I declare revelation is my portion, in Jesus's name.

Become a Sharpshooter in the Spirit

$\mathcal{I}$ am creating sharpshooters in the spirit that hit their target the first time around. You will become sharper and sharper and sharper as you exercise and train for a lifestyle of spiritual warfare. Practice with the weapons I've given you. Strap on the armor that I've put upon you. Like lifting heavy weights, you will grow sharper as you exercise, as you push, as you press. You will become stronger and sharper and more deadly to the kingdom of darkness.

JUDGES 20:16; 1 SAMUEL 17:49–50; EPHESIANS 6:11–18

PRAYER

Father, make me a sharpshooter in the spirit so I hit the devil between his eyes with the first release of my spiritual weapons. Help me cultivate an accurate spirit.

DECREE

I decree my eye is keen and my shot is accurate, blowing holes through the enemy's agenda. I declare my armor is impenetrable and God is my shield, in Jesus's name.

I Will Grace You to Keep Marching

I will give you the strength to march forward just like I gave you the strength to stand. Even though it feels like your feet are heavy and your thighs are burning, and even though you don't see clearly where you're going, I will give you the grace to keep going. I will extend your vision, and I will even cause you to see clearly in the midnight hour as you sing My praises. The scales will begin to fall off from the past season of weariness. The scales will begin to fall off from the lies that you received from the wicked one. The scales will begin to fall off, and you will begin to see and know which way to go.

2 CORINTHIANS 12:8–9; JAMES 4:6; 1 CORINTHIANS 15:10

PRAYER

Father, grace me to march and keep on marching. Extend my vision and bring clarity of mind so I can blast through the barrage of lies coming at my soul.

DECREE

I decree monitoring spirits are blinded and cannot peep into my life. I declare I have X-ray vision and can see through the lies of the enemy, in Jesus's name.

You Are Not Alone in the Fight

*Y*ou are not alone in the warfare—or in life. When you feel isolated and alone in the battle, remember that I will be with you just as I was with Moses and Joshua and Jesus. I know it can feel at times like I have forsaken you. But your feelings are not facts and facts are not truth. The truth is I am with you even if the facts defy My promise. I have promised never to leave you or forsake you, even to the end of the age. Don't look around to see that no one is standing with you. Look at Me.

ROMANS 8:35–39; JOSHUA 1:5; HEBREWS 13:5

PRAYER

Thank You, Lord, for reminding me that I am not fighting alone. Help me remember that You are always with Me all the time, forever.

DECREE

I decree heavenly resources are backing me up against all satanic backlash. I declare the Lord is a warrior and He is in me and I am in Him, in Jesus's name.

Don't Be Deceived

The enemy works in deception. He works at all points to deceive you. There is a battle of truth raging in the earth, and vain imaginations will attack your mind, weary your soul, and work to bend your will. This is why I have given you My Word and My belt of truth. This is why I have left you the sword of the Spirit, to cut through the lies of the enemy. Don't allow the enemy to deceive you. Stick with what I have said, not what things look like with your natural eyes. Again, I say, don't be deceived.

EPHESIANS 5:11; EPHESIANS 6:14; PSALM 25:5

PRAYER

Father, help me cut through the lies of the enemy with Your sword, which never grows dull. Sharpen my senses and help me rightly divide truth from lies.

DECREE

I decree the mischief of the enemy's lips covers him with darkness. I declare the words of my mouth will utter truth that sets me free and binds the enemy, in Jesus's name.

Deactivate the Enemy's Will for Your Life

*F*ully engage in the battle coming against your mind and you will win. Even though circumstances all around you appear to defy My will, you must remember I have promised to work all things together for your good. Stop staring at the circumstances and start speaking My will. Start resisting the thoughts the enemy is whispering in your ear and get vocal. Activate My will in your life by voicing My Word. Activate My will in your life by voicing My will. You will win the battle coming against your mind by opening your mouth and combating the vain imaginations. Speak the Word only.

ROMANS 8:28; MARK 11:24; JAMES 4:7

PRAYER

Father, help me fully engage in the battle at hand and not fight half-heartedly but fight with full confidence that You have strengthened me for such a time as this.

DECREE

I decree out-of-order circumstances in my life fall into line with God's Word now. I declare God's will is activated in my life when I speak His Word, in Jesus's name.

I Am Calling Companies of Spiritual Warriors

$\mathcal{R}$ise up now and find those who will war with you and for you and for whom you are willing to war with and for. I am calling companies of spiritual warriors to rise up and make a push into the kingdom of darkness, to bring light that blinds the enemy, to do what none of you could do alone but what you could accomplish together quite easily by faith. You will form battalions that break down the enemy's plans and bring breakthrough to many.

2 SAMUEL 23:8–38; GENESIS 14:14; JUDGES 7:17–22

PRAYER

Father, help me find my company of like precious faith so I can run to them in the battle and defend them in the war. Connect me with the breakthrough army.

DECREE

I decree angelic harassment on the hordes of demons raging against my life. I declare victory for warring companies of laid-down lovers sold out to Christ, in Jesus's name.

December 19

Embrace the Truth That Sets You Free

*R*eplace what's in your mind now—the thoughts, the worries, the concerns—with My Word. I've not called you to walk in the deception and double-mindedness the devil introduces to your soul. I've not called you to walk in the worry and fretting and overwhelming suggestions the enemy whispers to your heart. I've called you to walk in victory. Even though you know My truth, remember it's the truth you walk in, move in, meditate on, and speak out of your mouth that sets you free. Speak the truth!

JOHN 14:6; JOHN 8:32; JOHN 16:13

PRAYER

Father, I don't want to be double-minded and deceive myself. Break every everything that resembles double-mindedness off my life and help me walk circumspectly.

DECREE

I decree double-mindedness into the enemy's camp so demon forces cannot agree on a method of attack against me. I declare I am sober-minded and stable, in Jesus's name.

There Is Protection in Abiding

When you abide in Me and My Word abides in you, you can ask Me anything and I'll do it for you. No enemy can successfully oppose you. There is protection in My Word. There is freedom in the abiding. It's time to get out of the mental ascent mode and into give-me-more-revelation-of-Your-Word mode. It's time to get out of your mind and into My heart. It's time to get out head knowledge and into the heart revelation. It will cost you something, but it will be worth it to watch the enemy fall.

JOHN 5:1–10; 1 JOHN 2:6; 1 JOHN 2:27

PRAYER

Father, teach me the value of abiding, truly abiding in Your Word so I can walk in Your will and find total protection in Your presence. Show me the better way.

DECREE

I decree the enemy is forbidden to abide in my mind, my body, my home, or my family. I declare enemy revelation cannot penetrate my helmet of salvation, in Jesus's name.

I Am Your Victory Banner

𝒴ou are not to bow to the enemy, his threats, his temptations, or his plans. You are to bow to Me, the One who gives you victory. Don't keep bowing your knee to the one who wants to force you into utter devastation, into utter defeat, and into utter shame, but bow the knee to Me. Surrender to Me, the One who is your victory banner. For I will not leave you or forsake you in the battle. But you must know and understand that the victory is already secured.

DEUTERONOMY 20:4; PSALM 108:13; ISAIAH 41:3

PRAYER

Father, thank You for manifesting my victory in Christ before the enemy ever made his first move. Help me embrace the victorious work of the cross.

DECREE

I decree every wicked foe must surrender to me as Christ's ambassador and in His name. I declare my surrender to the Lord is deeper every day, in Jesus's name.

December 22

Think About My Love

Think things in your heart that I've said about you in My Word. Think of your victory and think of your breakthrough and think of your healing and think of your prosperity and think of your prodigals coming home and think of Me, for I love you. Think about My love. Think about the peace I promised you. Think about the joy unspeakable and glory that is ordained for you. Think about what I have said in the past seasons. Make a divine exchange—think My thoughts instead of the enemy's thoughts.

PSALM 10:29–31; PSALM 94:14

PRAYER

Father, help me recall what Your Word has said about me so my emotions can line up with Your thoughts toward me. Draw me close when the enemy tries to defy Your love.

DECREE

I decree every skewed mirror the enemy tempts me to gaze into shattered. I declare I walk in victory, healing, breakthrough, prosperity, and peace in Jesus's name.

The War to Enter the Door

There is indeed a war to go through the door I have ordained for your life. I will lead you and guide you. I will direct your steps to the threshold of your next conquest. You must walk with Me, and you must look at Me. You must take your cues and your signals from Me. I am speaking to you many times, and you do not hear because of the noise in the spirit, because of the enemy chatter, because of the doubts and the fears that are still in your own heart. Stop listening to these other voices and zoom in on Me, listen to Me, turn up My volume in your life and you will see and know that I can bring you right to the threshold and My hand on your hand will turn the knob on the door.

REVELATION 3:20; MATTHEW 7:7; JOHN 10:7–9

PRAYER

Father, strengthen me to war all the way through the door. Help my knuckles not to grow sore from the continual knocking. Direct my steps to the right thresholds.

DECREE

I decree the enemy's tormenting talk echoes back into his own rebellious ears. I declare all doorways of demonic entry in my life are sealed shut, in Jesus's name.

Get into My Rhythm

*M*any of My children are fellowshipping with the wicked one more than they are fellowshipping with Me. Don't listen to the enemy's promises, which indeed are masked threats against My promises. Instead meditate on My Word and what I've said to you in the past season. Who are you going to sup with? Who are you going to dine with? Who are you going to dance with? I want to be your dance partner and I want you to come into My rhythm and I want to sweep you off your feet. Stop getting into the demonic rhythms of your imaginations and begin to sing My song again because you can hear Me if you try, singing songs of deliverance over you.

2 CORINTHIANS 7:1; 1 JOHN 1:3; PSALM 30:11

PRAYER

Father, I choose to dance with You, to sing to You, to fellowship with You. Help me shut out demonic rhythms and get in synch with Your heart.

DECREE

I decree demonic chatter against my life is channeled back and to its satanic source. I declare my dance partner is the Elohim and I move in His timing, in Jesus's name.

December 25

Christ's Ultimate Act of Spiritual Warfare

*W*hen Christ died at Calvary it was the ultimate act of spiritual warfare. He went to war for your eternal soul by taking on your sin—the sin of the entire world. He felt the pain of separation from His heavenly Father, but He kept His eyes on the prize. He kept His eyes on you in the face of enemy attack. Now it's your turn. Get your mind off the pain the enemy has inflicted and get it on Jesus, the author and finisher of your faith and your victory banner. You'll win this battle.

PHILIPPIANS 3:14; HEBREWS 12:2; MATTHEW 6:22

PRAYER

Father, help me live a lifestyle of supernatural sacrifice so the world can see Jesus in me. Help me to withstand the warfare against my transformation in glory.

DECREE

I decree the enemy's intercession—and all witchcraft prayers against me—fall to the ground. I declare God has arranged for my win, in Jesus's name.

When You Feel Let Down and Held Up

I know you feel let down and held up at times. I know it's frustrating. Frustration can be deadly to your spiritual life. When you walk in frustration, you tend to walk in the flesh. When you walk in the flesh, you aren't walking in the Spirit. When you aren't walking in the Spirit, you are an open target for the enemy. Know and understand this: The enemy arranges circumstances to frustrate you so you will respond in the flesh instead of reacting by My Word and in My Spirit. Break the cycle.

ROMANS 5:3–5; GALATIANS 5:16; ROMANS 8:6

PRAYER

Father, help me never to frustrate Your grace, which is all-sufficient for every spiritual battle unto victory. Teach me to recognize and break demonic cycles.

DECREE

I decree frustration tactics bounce off my shield of faith. I declare I walk in the spirit of grace, move by the spirit of peace, and walk in the Word, in Jesus's name.

Make the Enemy's Head Spin

Gird up the loins of your mind. Have I not told you? Gird up the loins of your mind. Grab hold of your thought life. Be sober-minded. The enemy wants to disorient you with such incessant rapid-fire thoughts that you feel like your head is spinning. Toughen up. Shore up the weak areas of your mind. Determine not only in your heart but also determine in your soul that you will not fall for the same old lies. Then listen closely to your thoughts, My thoughts, and the enemy's thoughts and choose the better path. Make the enemy's head spin.

1 Peter 1:13; Philippians 2:5; Ephesians 4:22–24

PRAYER

Father, help me gird up the loins of my mind with Your Word so I am ready for battle when the enemy slithers into my jurisdiction with evil plots and plans.

DECREE

I decree the angelic interferences into the enemy's communication transmissions. I declare the devil's head spins with dismay when I release God's Word, in Jesus's name.

Guard Your Heart

Guard your heart, for out of it flow the issues of your life. If you don't guard your heart from the enemy's influence, you will find yourself sinning against Me and opening wide a door of attack against your mind. Guard your heart. Listen to what comes out of your mouth to locate what is in your heart. When you hear something out of line with My heart, repent. Change the way you think. Change your perspective. Guard your heart against the enemy's attempts to embitter you, tempt you into greed, and draw you into lust. Guard your heart.

PROVERBS 4:23; PSALM 51:10; PSALM 73:26

PRAYER

Father, set a guard over my mouth so I will not reveal to the wicked one the secret thoughts of my mind that don't line up with Your will. Help me guard my heart and mind.

DECREE

I decree every information-seeking spirit spying out my liberty and seeking to entrap me is bound. I declare my heart repents quickly for grievous words, in Jesus's name.

Pick Up Your Slingshot

$\mathcal{P}$ick up your slingshot. You don't need heavy artillery in every battle. The simple truths of My Word will take out every Goliath in your life. A sling and a stone can do great damage against the enemy. Sling My Word at his head. Sing My truth at his lie. Sling My light at his darkness. Sling My authority against his power. Pick up your slingshot. The enemy may taunt you and tempt you to pick up another weapon. But the reality is when he's slinging mud in your face, you can sling a deadly blow with a simple word of life in Christ's name.

1 Samuel 17:40; Judges 20:16; 1 Chronicles 12:2

PRAYER

Father, remind me to pick up my sling when the enemy is slinging mud at me. Help me wield the sling with accuracy to take out every Goliath in my life, in Jesus's name.

DECREE

I decree my spiritual sling knocks the devil on his back. I declare my supernatural weaponry is diverse and suitable to overcome for any and every battle, in Jesus's name.

I Am Raising Up Radicals

Radicals are rising to steal, kill, and destroy My plans and purposes in the earth—and in your life. Radical demons have wreaked havoc on churches, families, and individuals, bringing sickness, disease, poverty, and mind battles that have caused many to abandon their callings and abort their purposes. But I am blowing a radical wind of My Spirit on the willing in this season. I am raising up radical spiritual warriors who will operate in radical obedience and press past radical enemy assignments against radical breakthrough.

JOHN 10:10; 2 SAMUEL 23:8–39; ISAIAH 1:19–20

PRAYER

Father, thank You for warning me of the enemy's plans and purposes in the earth. Help me to prepare myself for every form and shape of weapon that assaults me.

DECREE

I decree the enemy's radical plans of destruction are reversed and redeployed to the enemy's dark camp. I declare my radical faith overcomes, in Jesus's name.

I Will Give You a New Beginning

*B*ehold, I do a new thing. Have you not seen it? Have you not heard it? Behold, I do a new thing. There is new wine. There are fresh starts and new beginnings. I am here now to meet you at the point of your determined decision to start over again. When you walk through a season where it seems everything that can go wrong does go wrong, know I am here to usher you into your new beginning. Even when the enemy encamps around you to do you harm, My angels are still there to keep you until it's time to step into your new season. Get ready for your fresh start.

ISAIAH 43:19; JOB 8:7; ECCLESIASTES 3:11

PRAYER

Father, thank You for the promise of all things new. Help me step into my new beginnings with faith and trust that my latter shall be greater than my past.

DECREE

I decree the doors to the past are shut and the enemy can no longer pull me into the pain of the past. I declare new beginnings are my portion, in Jesus's name.

About Jennifer LeClaire

Jennifer is senior leader of Awakening House of Prayer in Fort Lauderdale, FL, founder of the Ignite Network, and founder of the Awakening Blaze prayer movement. Jennifer formerly served as the first-ever female editor of *Charisma* magazine and is a prolific author of over 25 books.

You can find Jennifer online or shoot her an email at info@jenniferleclaire.org.